Building a Recommendation System with R

Learn the art of building robust and powerful recommendation engines using R

Suresh K. Gorakala

Michele Usuelli

open source
community experience distilled

BIRMINGHAM - MUMBAI

Building a Recommendation System with R

First published: September 2015

Production reference: 1240915

Published by Packt Publishing Ltd.
Livery Place
35 Livery Street
Birmingham B3 2PB, UK.

ISBN 978-1-78355-449-2

www.packtpub.com

Credits

Authors
Suresh K. Gorakala
Michele Usuelli

Reviewers
Ratanlal Mahanta
Cynthia O'Donnell

Commissioning Editor
Akram Hussain

Acquisition Editor
Usha Iyer

Content Development Editor
Kirti Patil

Technical Editor
Vijin Boricha

Copy Editors
Shruti Iyer
Karuna Narayanan

Project Coordinator
Kranti Berde

Proofreader
Safis Editing

Indexer
Mariammal Chettiyar

Graphics
Disha Haria

Production Coordinator
Conidon Miranda

Cover Work
Conidon Miranda

About the Authors

Suresh K. Gorakala is a blogger, data analyst, and consultant on data mining, big data analytics, and visualization tools. Since 2013, he has been writing and maintaining a blog on data science at `http://www.dataperspective.info/`.

Suresh holds a bachelor's degree in mechanical engineering from SRKR Engineering College, which is affiliated with Andhra University, India.

He loves generating ideas, building data products, teaching, photography, and travelling. Suresh can be reached at `sureshkumargorakala@gmail.com`. You can also follow him on Twitter at `@sureshgorakala`.

With great pleasure, I sincerely thank everyone who has supported me all along. I would like to thank my dad, my loving wife, and sister, who have supported me in all respects and without whom this book would not have been completed.

I am also grateful to my friends Rajesh, Hari, and Girish, who constantly support me and have stood by me in times of difficulty. I would like to extend a special thanks to Usha Iyer and Kirti Patil, who supported me in completing all my tasks. I would like to specially mention Michele Usuelli, without whom this book would be incomplete.

Michele Usuelli is a data scientist, writer, and R enthusiast specialized in the fields of big data and machine learning. He currently works for Revolution Analytics, the leading R-based company that got acquired by Microsoft in April 2015. Michele graduated in mathematical engineering and has worked with a big data start-up and a big publishing company in the past. He is also the author of *R Machine Learning Essentials*, *Packt Publishing*.

About the Reviewer

Ratanlal Mahanta has several years of experience in the modeling and simulation of quantitative trading. He works as a senior quantitative analyst at GPSK Investment Group, Kolkata. Ratanlal holds a master's degree of science in computational finance, and his research areas include quant trading, optimal execution, and high-frequency trading.

He has also reviewed *Mastering R for Quantitative Finance*, *Mastering Scientific Computing with R*, *Machine Learning with R Cookbook*, and *Mastering Python for Data Science*, all by Packt Publishing.

www.PacktPub.com

Support files, eBooks, discount offers, and more

For support files and downloads related to your book, please visit www.PacktPub.com.

Did you know that Packt offers eBook versions of every book published, with PDF and ePub files available? You can upgrade to the eBook version at www.PacktPub.com and as a print book customer, you are entitled to a discount on the eBook copy. Get in touch with us at service@packtpub.com for more details.

At www.PacktPub.com, you can also read a collection of free technical articles, sign up for a range of free newsletters and receive exclusive discounts and offers on Packt books and eBooks.

https://www2.packtpub.com/books/subscription/packtlib

Do you need instant solutions to your IT questions? PacktLib is Packt's online digital book library. Here, you can search, access, and read Packt's entire library of books.

Why subscribe?

- Fully searchable across every book published by Packt
- Copy and paste, print, and bookmark content
- On demand and accessible via a web browser

Free access for Packt account holders

If you have an account with Packt at www.PacktPub.com, you can use this to access PacktLib today and view 9 entirely free books. Simply use your login credentials for immediate access.

Dedicated in loving memory of my mother, Damayanti, whose world we were.

– Suresh K. Gorakala

Table of Contents

Preface

Recommender systems are machine learning techniques that predict user purchases and preferences. There are several applications of recommender systems, such as online retailers and video-sharing websites.

This book teaches the reader how to build recommender systems using R. It starts by providing the reader with some relevant data mining and machine learning concepts. Then, it shows how to build and optimize recommender models using R and gives an overview of the most popular recommendation techniques. In the end, it shows a practical use case. After reading this book, you will know how to build a new recommender system on your own.

What this book covers

Chapter 1, *Getting Started with Recommender Systems*, describes the book and presents some real-life examples of recommendation engines.

Chapter 2, *Data Mining Techniques Used in Recommender Systems*, provides the reader with the toolbox to built recommender models: R basics, data processing, and machine learning techniques.

Chapter 3, *Recommender Systems*, presents some popular recommender systems and shows how to build some of them using R.

Chapter 4, *Evaluating the Recommender Systems*, shows how to measure the performance of a recommender and how to optimize it.

Chapter 5, *Case Study – Building Your Own Recommendation Engine*, shows how to solve a business challenge by building and optimizing a recommender.

What you need for this book

You will need the R 3.0.0+, RStudio (not mandatory), and Samba 4.x Server software.

Who this book is for

This book is intended for people who already have a background in R and machine learning. If you're interested in building recommendation techniques, this book is for you.

Citation

To cite the `recommenderlab` package (R package version 0.1-5) in publications, refer to *recommenderlab: Lab for Developing and Testing Recommender Algorithms* by *Michael Hahsler* at `http://CRAN.R-project.org/package=recommenderlab`

LaTeX users can use the following BibTeX entry:

```
@Manual{,
    title = {recommenderlab: Lab for Developing and Testing
    Recommender Algorithms},
    author = {Michael Hahsler},
    year = {2014},
    note = {R package version 0.1-5},
    url = { http://CRAN.R-
    project.org/package=recommenderlab},
}
```

Conventions

In this book, you will find a number of text styles that distinguish between different kinds of information. Here are some examples of these styles and an explanation of their meaning.

Code words in text, database table names, folder names, filenames, file extensions, pathnames, dummy URLs, user input, and Twitter handles are shown as follows: "We used the `e1071` package to run SVM."

A block of code is set as follows:

```
vector_ratings <- factor(vector_ratings)
qplot(vector_ratings) + ggtitle("Distribution of the ratings")
exten => i,1,Voicemail(s0)
```

New terms and **important words** are shown in bold.

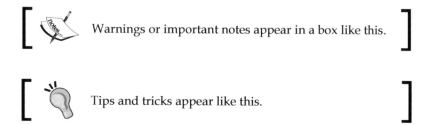

> Warnings or important notes appear in a box like this.

> Tips and tricks appear like this.

Reader feedback

Feedback from our readers is always welcome. Let us know what you think about this book—what you liked or disliked. Reader feedback is important for us as it helps us develop titles that you will really get the most out of.

To send us general feedback, simply e-mail feedback@packtpub.com, and mention the book's title in the subject of your message.

If there is a topic that you have expertise in and you are interested in either writing or contributing to a book, see our author guide at www.packtpub.com/authors.

Customer support

Now that you are the proud owner of a Packt book, we have a number of things to help you to get the most from your purchase.

Downloading the example code

You can download the example code files from your account at http://www.packtpub.com for all the Packt Publishing books you have purchased. If you purchased this book elsewhere, you can visit http://www.packtpub.com/support and register to have the files e-mailed directly to you.

Downloading the color images of this book

We also provide you with a PDF file that has color images of the screenshots/ diagrams used in this book. The color images will help you better understand the changes in the output. You can download this file from: `https://www.packtpub. com/sites/default/files/downloads/44920S_GraphicBundle.pdf`.

Errata

Although we have taken every care to ensure the accuracy of our content, mistakes do happen. If you find a mistake in one of our books—maybe a mistake in the text or the code—we would be grateful if you could report this to us. By doing so, you can save other readers from frustration and help us improve subsequent versions of this book. If you find any errata, please report them by visiting `http://www.packtpub. com/submit-errata`, selecting your book, clicking on the **Errata Submission Form** link, and entering the details of your errata. Once your errata are verified, your submission will be accepted and the errata will be uploaded to our website or added to any list of existing errata under the Errata section of that title.

To view the previously submitted errata, go to `https://www.packtpub.com/books/ content/support` and enter the name of the book in the search field. The required information will appear under the **Errata** section.

Piracy

Piracy of copyrighted material on the Internet is an ongoing problem across all media. At Packt, we take the protection of our copyright and licenses very seriously. If you come across any illegal copies of our works in any form on the Internet, please provide us with the location address or website name immediately so that we can pursue a remedy.

Please contact us at `copyright@packtpub.com` with a link to the suspected pirated material.

We appreciate your help in protecting our authors and our ability to bring you valuable content.

Questions

If you have a problem with any aspect of this book, you can contact us at `questions@packtpub.com`, and we will do our best to address the problem.

1
Getting Started with Recommender Systems

How do we buy things in our day-to-day lives? We ask our friends, research the product specifications, compare the product with similar products on the Internet, read the feedback from anonymous users, and then we make decisions. How would it be if there is some mechanism that does all these tasks automatically and recommends the products best suited for you efficiently? A recommender system or recommendation engine is the answer to this question.

In this introductory chapter, we will define a recommender system in terms of the following aspects:

- Helping to develop an understanding of its definition
- Explaining its basic functions and providing a general introduction of popular recommender systems
- Highlighting the importance of evaluation techniques

Understanding recommender systems

Have you ever given a thought to the "People you may know" feature in LinkedIn or Facebook? This feature recommends a list of people whom you might know, who are similar to you based on your friends, friends of friends in your close circle, geographical location, skillsets, groups, liked pages, and so on. These recommendations are specific to you and differ from user to user.

Recommender systems are the software tools and techniques that provide suggestions, such as useful products on e-commerce websites, videos on YouTube, friends' recommendations on Facebook, book recommendations on Amazon, news recommendations on online news websites, and the list goes on.

The main goal of recommender systems is to provide suggestions to online users to make better decisions from many alternatives available over the Web. A better recommender system is directed more towards personalized recommendations by taking into consideration the available digital footprint of the user and information about a product, such as specifications, feedback from the users, comparison with other products, and so on, before making recommendations.

The structure of the book

In this book, we will learn about popular recommender systems that are used the most. We will also look into different machine learning techniques used when building recommendation engines with sample code.

The book is divided into 5 chapters:

- In *Chapter 1, Getting Started with Recommender Systems*, you will get a general introduction to recommender systems, such as collaborative filtering recommender systems, content-based recommender systems, knowledge-based recommender systems, and hybrid systems; it will also include a brief definition, real-world examples, and brief details of what one will be learning while building a recommender system.

- In *Chapter 2, Data Mining Techniques Used in Recommender Systems*, gives you an overview of different machine learning concepts that are commonly used in building a recommender system and how a data analysis problem can be solved. This chapter includes data preprocessing techniques, such as similarity measures, dimensionality reduction, data mining techniques, and its evaluation techniques. Here similarity measures such as Euclidean distance, Cosine distance, Pearson correlation are explained. We will also cover data mining algorithms such as *k*-means clustering, support vector machines, decision trees, bagging, boosting, and random forests, along with a popular dimensional reduction technique, PCA. Evaluation techniques such as cross validation, regularization, confusion matrix, and model comparison are explained in brief.

- In *Chapter 3, Recommender Systems*, we will discuss collaborative filtering recommender systems, an example for user- and item-based recommender systems, using the `recommenderlab` R package, and the `MovieLens` dataset. We will cover model building, which includes exploring data, splitting it into train and test datasets, and dealing with binary ratings. You will have an overview of content-based recommender systems, knowledge-based recommender systems, and hybrid systems.

- In *Chapter 4, Evaluating the Recommender Systems*, we will learn about the evaluation techniques for recommender systems, such as setting up the evaluation, evaluating recommender systems, and optimizing the parameters.

- In *Chapter 5, Case Study – Building Your Own Recommendation Engine*, we will understand a use case in R, which includes steps such as preparing the data, defining the rating matrix, building a recommender, and evaluating and optimizing a recommender.

Collaborative filtering recommender systems

The basic idea of these systems is that, if two users share the same interests in the past, that is, they liked the same book, they will also have similar tastes in the future. If, for example, user A and user B have a similar purchase history and user A recently bought a book that user B has not yet seen, the basic idea is to propose this book to user B. The book recommendations on Amazon are one good example of this type of recommender system.

In this type of recommendation, filtering items from a large set of alternatives is done collaboratively between users preferences. Such systems are called collaborative filtering recommender systems.

While dealing with collaborative filtering recommender systems, we will learn about the following aspects:

- How to calculate the similarity between users
- How to calculate the similarity between items
- How do we deal with new items and new users whose data is not known

The collaborative filtering approach considers only user preferences and does not take into account the features or contents of the items being recommended. This approach requires a large set of user preferences for more accurate results.

Content-based recommender systems

This system recommends items to users by taking the similarity of items and user profiles into consideration. In simpler terms, the system recommends items similar to those that the user has liked in the past. The similarity of items is calculated based on the features associated with the other compared items and is matched with the user's historical preferences.

As an example, we can assume that, if a user has positively rated a movie that belongs to the action genre, then the system can learn to recommend other movies from the action genre.

While building a content-based recommendation system, we take into consideration the following questions:

- How do we create similarity between items?
- How do we create and update user profiles continuously?

This technique doesn't take into consideration the user's neighborhood preferences. Hence, it doesn't require a large user group's preference for items for better recommendation accuracy. It only considers the user's past preferences and the properties/features of the items.

Knowledge-based recommender systems

These types of recommender systems are employed in specific domains where the purchase history of the users is smaller. In such systems, the algorithm takes into consideration the knowledge about the items, such as features, user preferences asked explicitly, and recommendation criteria, before giving recommendations. The accuracy of the model is judged based on how useful the recommended item is to the user. Take, for example, a scenario in which you are building a recommender system that recommends household electronics, such as air conditioners, where most of the users will be first timers. In this case, the system considers features of the items, and user profiles are generated by obtaining additional information from the users, such as specifications, and then recommendations are made. These types of system are called constraint-based recommender systems, which we will learn more about in subsequent chapters.

Before building these types of recommender systems, we take into consideration the following questions:

- What kind of information about the items is taken into the model?
- How are user preferences captured explicitly?

Hybrid systems

We build hybrid recommender systems by combining various recommender systems to build a more robust system. By combining various recommender systems, we can eliminate the disadvantages of one system with the advantages of another system and thus build a more robust system. For example, by combining collaborative filtering methods, where the model fails when new items don't have ratings, with content-based systems, where feature information about the items is available, new items can be recommended more accurately and efficiently.

Before building a hybrid model, we consider the following questions:

- What techniques should be combined to achieve the business solution?
- How should we combine various techniques and their results for better predictions?

Evaluation techniques

Before rolling out the recommender system to the users, how do we ensure that the system is efficient or accurate? What is the base on which we state that the system is good? As stated earlier, the goal of any recommendation system is to recommend more relevant and useful items to the user. A lot of research has been happening in developing new methods to evaluate the recommender systems to improve the accuracy of the systems.

In *Chapter 4, Evaluating the Recommender Systems*, we will learn about the different evaluation metrics employed to evaluate the recommender systems, these include setting up the evaluation, evaluating recommender systems, optimizing the parameters. This chapter also focuses on how important evaluating the system is during the design and development phases of building recommender systems and the guidelines to be followed in selecting an algorithm based on the available information about the items and the problem statement. This chapter also covers the different experimental setups in which recommender systems are evaluated.

A case study

In *Chapter 5, Case Study – Building Your Own Recommendation Engine*, we take a case study and build a recommender system step by step as follows:

1. We take a real-life case and understand the problem statement and its domain aspects

2. We then perform the data preparation, data source identification, and data cleansing step

3. Then, we select an algorithm for the recommender system

4. We then look into the design and development aspects while building the model

5. Finally, we evaluate and test the recommender system

The implementation of the recommender system is done using R, and code samples will be provided in the book. At the end of this chapter, you will be confident enough to build your own recommendation engine.

The future scope

In the final chapter, I will wrap up by giving the summary of the book and the topics covered. We will focus on the future scope of the research that you will have to undertake. Then we will provide a brief introduction to the current research topics and advancements happening in the field of recommendation systems. I will also list book references and online resources during the course of this book.

Summary

In this chapter, you read a synopsis of the popular recommender systems available on the market. In the next chapter, you will learn about the different machine learning techniques used in recommender systems.

2

Data Mining Techniques Used in Recommender Systems

Though the primary objective of this book is to build recommender systems, a walkthrough of the commonly used data-mining techniques is a necessary step before jumping into building recommender systems. In this chapter, you will learn about popular data preprocessing techniques, data-mining techniques, and data-evaluation techniques commonly used in recommender systems. The first section of the chapter tells you how a data analysis problem is solved, followed by data preprocessing steps such as similarity measures and dimensionality reduction. The next section of the chapter deals with data mining techniques and their evaluation techniques.

Similarity measures include:

- Euclidean distance
- Cosine distance
- Pearson correlation

Dimensionality reduction techniques include:

- Principal component analysis

Data-mining techniques include:

- k-means clustering
- Support vector machine
- Ensemble methods, such as bagging, boosting, and random forests

Solving a data analysis problem

Any data analysis problem involves a series of steps such as:

- Identifying a business problem.

- Understanding the problem domain with the help of a domain expert.

- Identifying data sources and data variables suitable for the analysis.

- Data preprocessing or a cleansing step, such as identifying missing values, quantitative and qualitative variables and transformations, and so on.

- Performing exploratory analysis to understand the data, mostly through visual graphs such as box plots or histograms.

- Performing basic statistics such as mean, median, modes, variances, standard deviations, correlation among the variables, and covariance to understand the nature of the data.

- Dividing the data into training and testing datasets and running a model using machine-learning algorithms with training datasets, using cross-validation techniques.

- Validating the model using the test data to evaluate the model on the new data. If needed, improve the model based on the results of the validation step.

- Visualize the results and deploy the model for real-time predictions.

The following image displays the resolution to a data analysis problem:

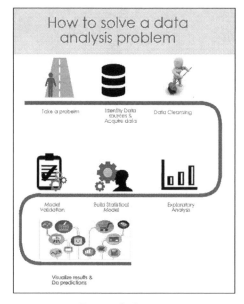

Data analysis steps

Data preprocessing techniques

Data preprocessing is a crucial step for any data analysis problem. The model's accuracy depends mostly on the quality of the data. In general, any data preprocessing step involves data cleansing, transformations, identifying missing values, and how they should be treated. Only the preprocessed data can be fed into a machine-learning algorithm. In this section, we will focus mainly on data preprocessing techniques. These techniques include similarity measurements (such as Euclidean distance, Cosine distance, and Pearson coefficient) and dimensionality-reduction techniques, such as **Principal component analysis (PCA)**, which are widely used in recommender systems. Apart from PCA, we have **singular value decomposition (SVD)**, subset feature selection methods to reduce the dimensions of the dataset, but we limit our study to PCA.

Similarity measures

As discussed in the previous chapter, every recommender system works on the concept of similarity between items or users. In this section, let's explore some similarity measures such as Euclidian distance, Cosine distance, and Pearson correlation.

Euclidian distance

The simplest technique for calculating the similarity between two items is by calculating its Euclidian distance. The Euclidean distance between two points/ objects (point x and point y) in a dataset is defined by the following equation:

$$\text{Euclidean Distance}(x, y) = \sqrt{\sum_{i=1}^{n} |x_i - y_i|^2}$$

In this equation, (x, y) are two consecutive data points, and n is the number of attributes for the dataset.

R script to calculate the Euclidean distance is as follows:

```
x1 <- rnorm(30)
x2 <- rnorm(30)
Euc_dist = dist(rbind(x1,x2) ,method="euclidean")
```

Cosine distance

Cosine similarity is a measure of similarity between two vectors of an inner product space that measures the cosine of the angle between them. Cosine similarity is given by this equation:

$$\text{similarity} = \cos(\theta) = \frac{A \cdot B}{\|A\|\|B\|}$$

R script to calculate the cosine distance is as follows:

```
vec1 = c( 1, 1, 1, 0, 0, 0, 0, 0, 0, 0, 0, 0 )
vec2 = c( 0, 0, 1, 1, 1, 1, 1, 0, 1, 0, 0, 0 )
library(lsa)
cosine(vec1,vec2)
```

In this equation, x is the matrix containing all variables in a dataset. The `cosine` function is available in the `lsa` package.

Pearson correlation

Similarity between two products can also be given by the correlation existing between their variables. Pearson's correlation coefficient is a popular correlation coefficient calculated between two variables as the covariance of the two variables divided by the product of their standard deviations. This is given by *p (rho)*:

$$\rho_{X,Y} = \frac{\text{cov}(X,Y)}{\sigma_X \sigma_Y}$$

R script is given by these lines of code:

```
Coef = cor(mtcars, method="pearson")
where mtcars is the dataset
```

Empirical studies showed that Pearson coefficient outperformed other similarity measures for user-based collaborative filtering recommender systems. The studies also show that Cosine similarity consistently performs well in item-based collaborative filtering.

Dimensionality reduction

One of the most commonly faced problems while building recommender systems is high-dimensional and sparse data. At many times, we face a situation where we have a large set of features and fewer data points. In such situations, when we fit a model to the dataset, the predictive power of the model will be lower. This scenario is often termed as the curse of dimensionality. In general, adding more data points or decreasing the feature space, also known as dimensionality reduction, often reduces the effects of the curse of dimensionality. In this chapter, we will discuss PCA, a popular dimensionality reduction technique to reduce the effects of the curse of dimensionality.

Principal component analysis

Principal component analysis is a classical statistical technique for dimensionality reduction. The PCA algorithm transforms the data with high-dimensional space to a space with fewer dimensions. The algorithm linearly transforms m-dimensional input space to n-dimensional ($n<m$) output space, with the objective to minimize the amount of information/variance lost by discarding (m-n) dimensions. PCA allows us to discard the variables/features that have less variance.

Technically speaking, PCA uses orthogonal projection of highly correlated variables to a set of values of linearly uncorrelated variables called principal components. The number of principal components is less than or equal to the number of original variables. This linear transformation is defined in such a way that the first principal component has the largest possible variance. It accounts for as much of the variability in the data as possible by considering highly correlated features. Each succeeding component in turn has the highest variance using the features that are less correlated with the first principal component and that are orthogonal to the preceding component.

Let's understand this in simple terms. Assume we have three dimensional data space with two features more correlated with each other than with the third. We now want to reduce the data to two-dimensional space using PCA. The first principal component is created in such a way that it explains maximum variance using the two correlated variables along the data. In the following graph, the first principal component (bigger line) is along the data explaining most variance. To choose the second principal component, we need to choose another line that has the highest variance, is uncorrelated, and is orthogonal to the first principal component. The implementation and technical details of PCA are beyond the scope of this book, so we will discuss how it is used in R.

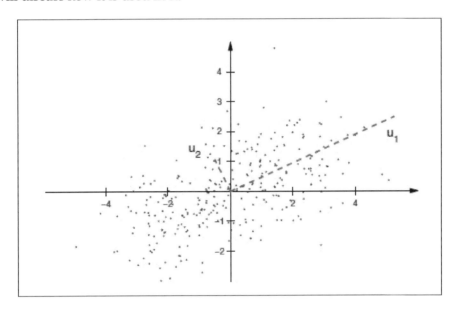

We will illustrate PCA using the USArrests dataset. The USArrests dataset contains crime-related statistics, such as Assault, Murder, Rape, and UrbanPop per 100,000 residents in 50 states in the US:

```
#PCA
data(USArrests)
head(states)
[1] "Alabama"    "Alaska"     "Arizona"    "Arkansas"    "California"
"Colorado"

names(USArrests)
[1] "Murder"    "Assault"   "UrbanPop"  "Rape"

#let us use apply() to the USArrests dataset row wise to calculate the
variance to see how each variable is varying
```

```
apply(USArrests , 2, var)
```

```
Murder    Assault   UrbanPop      Rape
  18.97047 6945.16571  209.51878   87.72916
```
#We observe that Assault has the most variance. It is important to note at this point that

#Scaling the features is a very step while applying PCA.

#Applying PCA after scaling the feature as below
```
pca =prcomp(USArrests , scale =TRUE)
```

```
pca
```

Standard deviations:

```
[1]  1.5748783 0.9948694 0.5971291 0.4164494
```

Rotation:

```
                 PC1         PC2        PC3         PC4
Murder    -0.5358995  0.4181809 -0.3412327  0.64922780
Assault   -0.5831836  0.1879856 -0.2681484 -0.74340748
UrbanPop  -0.2781909 -0.8728062 -0.3780158  0.13387773
Rape      -0.5434321 -0.1673186  0.8177779  0.08902432
```

#Now lets us understand the components of pca output.

```
names(pca)
[1] "sdev"      "rotation" "center"    "scale"    "x"
```

#Pca$rotation contains the principal component loadings matrix which explains

#proportion of each variable along each principal component.

#now let us learn interpreting the results of pca using biplot graph. Biplot is used to how the proportions of each variable along the two principal components.

#below code changes the directions of the biplot, if we donot include the below two lines the plot will be mirror image to the below one.
```
pca$rotation=-pca$rotation
pca$x=-pca$x
biplot (pca , scale =0)
```

The output of the preceding code is as follows:

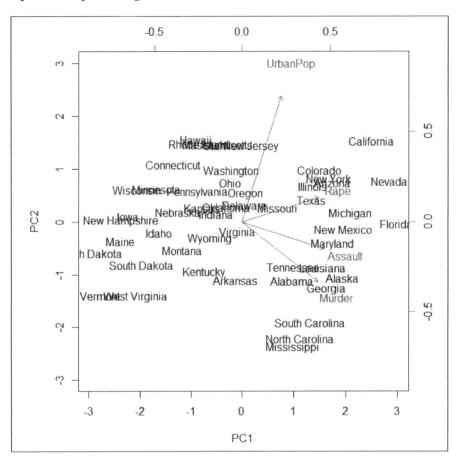

In the preceding image, known as a biplot, we can see the two principal components (**PC1** and **PC2**) of the USArrests dataset. The red arrows represent the loading vectors, which represent how the feature space varies along the principal component vectors.

From the plot, we can see that the first principal component vector, **PC1**, more or less places equal weight on three features: **Rape**, **Assault**, and **Murder**. This means that these three features are more correlated with each other than the **UrbanPop** feature. In the second principal component, **PC2** places more weight on **UrbanPop** than the remaining 3 features are less correlated with them.

Data mining techniques

In this section, we will look at commonly used data-mining algorithms, such as k-means clustering, support vector machines, decision trees, bagging, boosting, and random forests. Evaluation techniques such as cross validation, regularization, confusion matrix, and model comparison are explained in brief.

Cluster analysis

Cluster analysis is the process of grouping objects together in a way that objects in one group are more similar than objects in other groups.

An example would be identifying and grouping clients with similar booking activities on a travel portal, as shown in the following figure.

In the preceding example, each group is called a cluster, and each member (data point) of the cluster behaves in a manner similar to its group members.

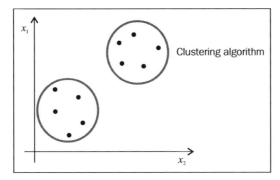

Cluster analysis

Cluster analysis is an unsupervised learning method. In supervised methods, such as regression analysis, we have input variables and response variables. We fit a statistical model to the input variables to predict the response variable. Whereas in unsupervised learning methods, however, we do not have any response variable to predict; we only have input variables. Instead of fitting a model to the input variables to predict the response variable, we just try to find patterns within the dataset. There are three popular clustering algorithms: hierarchical cluster analysis, k-means cluster analysis, and two-step cluster analysis. In the following section, we will learn about k-means clustering.

Explaining the k-means cluster algorithm

k-means is an unsupervised, iterative algorithm where k is the number of clusters to be formed from the data. Clustering is achieved in two steps:

1. **Cluster assignment step**: In this step, we randomly choose two cluster points (red dot and green dot) and assign each data point to the cluster point that is closer to it (top part of the following image).

2. **Move centroid step**: In this step, we take the average of the points of all the examples in each group and move the centroid to the new position, that is, mean position calculated (bottom part of the following image).

The preceding steps are repeated until all the data points are grouped into two groups and the mean of the data points after moving the centroid doesn't change.

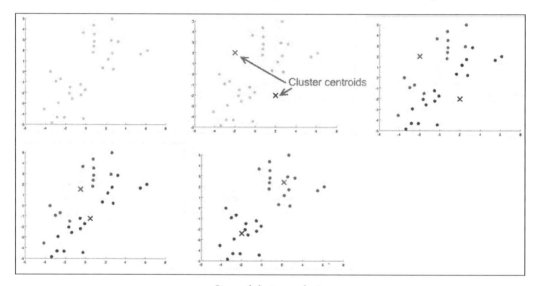

Steps of cluster analysis

The preceding image shows how a clustering algorithm works on data to form clusters. See the R implementation of *k*-means clustering on iris dataset as follows:

```
#k-means clustering
library(cluster)
data(iris)
iris$Species = as.numeric(iris$Species)
kmeans<- kmeans(x=iris, centers=5)
clusplot(iris,kmeans$cluster, color=TRUE, shade=TRUE,labels=13,
lines=0)
```

The output of the preceding code is as follows:

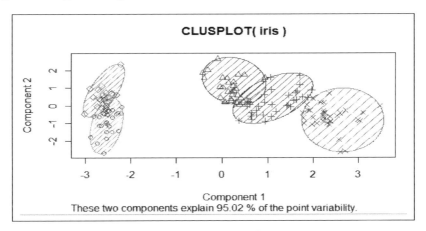

Cluster analysis results

The preceding image shows the formation of clusters on the iris data, and the clusters account for 95 percent of the data. In the preceding example, the number of clusters of *k* value is selected using the `elbow` method, as shown here:

```
library(cluster)
library(ggplot2)
data(iris)
iris$Species = as.numeric(iris$Species)
cost_df <- data.frame()
for(i in 1:100){
kmeans<- kmeans(x=iris, centers=i, iter.max=50)
cost_df<- rbind(cost_df, cbind(i, kmeans$tot.withinss))
}
names(cost_df) <- c("cluster", "cost")
#Elbow method to identify the idle number of Cluster
#Cost plot
ggplot(data=cost_df, aes(x=cluster, y=cost, group=1)) +
theme_bw(base_family="Garamond") +
geom_line(colour = "darkgreen") +
theme(text = element_text(size=20)) +
ggtitle("Reduction In Cost For Values of 'k'\n") +
xlab("\nClusters") +
ylab("Within-Cluster Sum of Squares\n")
```

The following image shows the cost reduction for *k* values:

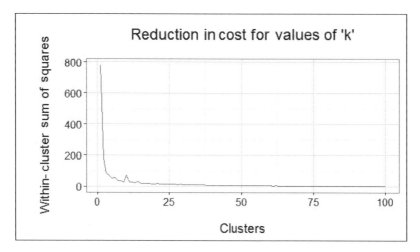

From the preceding figure, we can observe that the direction of the cost function is changed at cluster number 5. Hence, we choose 5 as our number of clusters k. Since the number of optimal clusters is found at the elbow of the graph, we call it the elbow method.

Support vector machine

Support vector machine algorithms are a form of supervised learning algorithms employed to solve classification problems. SVM is generally treated as one of the best algorithms to deal with classification problems. Given a set of training examples, where each data point falls into one of two categories, an SVM training algorithm builds a model that assigns new data points into one category or the other. This model is a representation of the examples as a points in space, mapped so that the examples of the separate categories are divided by a margin that is as wide as possible, as shown in the following image. New examples are then mapped into that same space and predicted to belong to a category based on which side of the gap they fall on. In this section, we will go through an overview and implementation of SVMs without going into mathematical details.

When SVM is applied to a p-dimensional dataset, the data is mapped to a *p-1* dimensional hyperplane, and the algorithm finds a clear boundary with a sufficient margin between classes. Unlike other classification algorithms that also create a separating boundary to classify data points, SVM tries to choose a boundary that has the maximum margin to separate the classes, as shown in the following image:

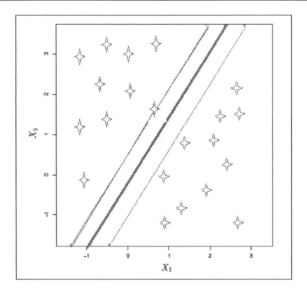

Consider a two-dimensional dataset having two classes, as shown in the preceding image. Now, when the SVM algorithm is applied, first it checks whether a one-dimensional hyperplane exists to map all the data points. If the hyperplane exists, the linear classifier creates a decision boundary with a margin to separate the classes. In the preceding image, the thick red line is the decision boundary, and the thinner blue and red lines are the margins of each class from the boundary. When new test data is used to predict the class, the new data falls into one of the two classes.

Here are some key points to be noted:

- Though an infinite number of hyperplanes can be created, SVM chooses only one hyperplane that has the maximum margin, that is, the separating hyperplane that is farthest from the training observations.

- This classifier is only dependent on the data points that lie on the margins of the hyperplane, that is, on thin margins in the image, but not on other observations in the dataset. These points are called support vectors.

- The decision boundary is affected only by the support vectors but not by other observations located away from the boundaries. If we change the data points other than the support vectors, there would not be any effect on the decision boundary. However, if the support vectors are changed, the decision boundary changes.

- A large margin on the training data will also have a large margin on the test data to classify the test data correctly.

- Support vector machines also perform well with non-linear datasets. In this case, we use radial kernel functions.

See the R implementation of SVM on the iris dataset in the following code snippet. We used the `e1071` package to run SVM. In R, the `SVM()` function contains the implementation of support vector machines present in the `e1071` package.

Now, we will see that the `SVM()` method is called with the `tune()` method, which does cross validation and runs the model on different values of the cost parameters.

The cross-validation method is used to evaluate the accuracy of the predictive model before testing on future unseen data:

```
   #SVM
library(e1071)
data(iris)
sample = iris[sample(nrow(iris)),]
train = sample[1:105,]
test = sample[106:150,]
tune =tune(svm,Species~.,data=train,kernel
="radial",scale=FALSE,ranges =list(cost=c(0.001,0.01,0.1,1,5,10,100)))
tune$best.model
```

Call:

```
best.tune(method = svm, train.x = Species ~ ., data = train, ranges =
list(cost = c(0.001,
    0.01, 0.1, 1, 5, 10, 100)), kernel = "radial", scale = FALSE)
```

Parameters:

```
    SVM-Type:  C-classification
 SVM-Kernel:  radial
       cost:  10
      gamma:  0.25


Number of Support Vectors:   25


summary(tune)


Parameter tuning of 'svm':
- sampling method: 10-fold cross validation
- best parameters:
 cost
   10
- best performance: 0.02909091
- Detailed performance results:
    cost       error dispersion
1 1e-03 0.72909091 0.20358585
```

```
2 1e-02 0.72909091 0.20358585
3 1e-01 0.04636364 0.08891242
4 1e+00 0.04818182 0.06653568
5 5e+00 0.03818182 0.06538717
6 1e+01 0.02909091 0.04690612
7 1e+02 0.07636364 0.08679584
```

```
model =svm(Species~.,data=train,kernel ="radial",cost=10,scale=FALSE)
// cost =10 is chosen from summary result of tune variable
```

The `tune$best.model` object tells us that the model works best with the cost parameter as `10` and total number of support vectors as `25`:

```
pred = predict(model,test)
```

Decision trees

Decision trees are a simple, fast, tree-based supervised learning algorithm to solve classification problems. Though not very accurate when compared to other logistic regression methods, this algorithm comes in handy while dealing with recommender systems.

We define the decision trees with an example. Imagine a situation where you have to predict the class of flower based on its features such as petal length, petal width, sepal length, and sepal width. We will apply the decision tree methodology to solve this problem:

1. Consider the entire data at the start of the algorithm.

2. Now, choose a suitable question/variable to divide the data into two parts. In our case, we chose to divide the data based on petal length > 2.45 and <= 2.45. This separates flower class `setosa` from the rest of the classes.

3. Now, further divide the data having petal length >2.45, based on the same variable with petal length < 4.5 and >= 4.5, as shown in the following image.

4. This splitting of the data will be further divided by narrowing down the data space until we reach a point where all the bottom points represent the response variables or where further logical split cannot be done on the data.

In the following decision tree image, we have one root node, four internal nodes where data split occurred, and five terminal nodes where data split cannot be done any further. They are defined as follows:

- **Petal.Length <2.45** as root node

- **Petal.Length <4.85, Sepal.Length <5.15,** and **Petal.Width <1.75** are called internal nodes

- Final nodes having the class of the flowers are called terminal nodes
- The lines connecting the nodes are called the branches of the tree

While predicting responses on new data using the previously built model, each new data point is taken through each node, a question is asked, and a logical path is taken to reach its logical class, as shown in the following figure:

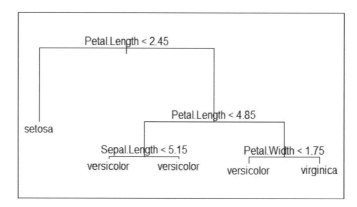

See the decision tree implementation in R on the iris dataset using the tree package available from **Comprehensive R Archive Network (CRAN)**.

The summary of the mode is given here. It tells us that the misclassification rate is 0.0381, indicating that the model is accurate:

```
library(tree)
data(iris)
sample = iris[sample(nrow(iris)),]
train = sample[1:105,]
test = sample[106:150,]
model = tree(Species~.,train)
summary(model)
```

Classification tree:

```
tree(formula = Species ~ ., data = train, x = TRUE, y = TRUE)
Variables actually used in tree construction:
[1] "Petal.Length" "Sepal.Length" "Petal.Width"
Number of terminal nodes:  5
Residual mean deviance:  0.1332 = 13.32 / 100
Misclassification error rate: 0.0381 = 4 / 105 '
//plotting the decision tree
plot(model)text(model)
pred = predict(model,test[,-5],type="class")
```

```
> pred
 [1] setosa      setosa      virginica  setosa      setosa      setosa
versicolor
 [8] virginica  virginica   setosa      versicolor versicolor virginica
versicolor
[15] virginica  virginica   setosa      virginica  virginica  versicolor
virginica
[22] versicolor setosa      virginica  setosa      versicolor virginica
setosa
[29] versicolor versicolor versicolor virginica  setosa      virginica
virginica
[36] versicolor setosa      versicolor setosa      versicolor versicolor
setosa
[43] versicolor setosa      setosa
Levels: setosa versicolor virginica
```

Ensemble methods

In data mining, we use ensemble methods, which means using multiple learning algorithms to obtain better predictive results than applying any single learning algorithm on any statistical problem. This section will provide an overview of popular ensemble methods such as bagging, boosting, and random forests

Bagging

Bagging is also known as Bootstrap aggregating. It is designed to improve the stability and accuracy of machine-learning algorithms. It helps avoid over fitting and reduces variance. This is mostly used with decision trees.

Bagging involves randomly generating Bootstrap samples from the dataset and trains the models individually. Predictions are then made by aggregating or averaging all the response variables:

- For example, consider a dataset (X_i, Y_i), where $i=1 \ldots n$, contains n data points.

- Now, randomly select B samples with replacements from the original dataset using Bootstrap technique.

- Next, train the B samples with regression/classification models independently. Then, predictions are made on the test set by averaging the responses from all the B models generated in the case of regression. Alternatively, the most often occurring class among B samples is generated in the case of classification.

Random forests

Random forests are improvised supervised algorithms than bootstrap aggregation or bagging methods, though they are built on a similar approach. Unlike selecting all the variables in all the B samples generated using the Bootstrap technique in bagging, we select only a few predictor variables randomly from the total variables for each of the B samples. Then, these samples are trained with the models. Predictions are made by averaging the result of each model. The number of predictors in each sample is decided using the formula $m = \sqrt{p}$, where p is the total variable count in the original dataset.

Here are some key notes:

- This approach removes the condition of dependency of strong predictors in the dataset as we intentionally select fewer variables than all the variables for every iteration
- This approach also de-correlates variables, resulting in less variability in the model and, hence, more reliability

Refer to the R implementation of random forests on the iris dataset using the randomForest package available from CRAN:

```
#randomForest
library(randomForest)
data(iris)
sample = iris[sample(nrow(iris)),]
train = sample[1:105,]
test = sample[106:150,]
model =randomForest(Species~.,data=train,mtry=2,importance
=TRUE,proximity=TRUE)
model
```

Call:

```
 randomForest(formula = Species ~ ., data = train, mtry = 2,
importance = TRUE,        proximity = TRUE)
               Type of random forest: classification
                     Number of trees: 500
No. of variables tried at each split: 2

        OOB estimate of  error rate: 5.71%
Confusion matrix:
           setosa versicolor virginica class.error
setosa         40          0         0  0.00000000
versicolor      0         28         3  0.09677419
virginica       0          3        31  0.08823529
```

```
pred = predict(model,newdata=test[,-5])
pred
pred
```

	119	77	88	90	51	20
96						
	virginica	versicolor	versicolor	versicolor	versicolor	setosa
versicolor						
	1	3	118	127	6	102
5						
	setosa	setosa	virginica	virginica	setosa	virginica
setosa						
	91	8	23	133	17	78
52						
versicolor		setosa	setosa	virginica	setosa	virginica
versicolor						
	63	82	84	116	70	50
129						
versicolor	versicolor	virginica	virginica	versicolor		setosa
virginica						
	150	34	9	120	41	26
121						
	virginica	setosa	setosa	virginica	setosa	setosa
virginica						
	145	138	94	4	104	81
122						
	virginica	virginica	versicolor		setosa	virginica	versicolor
virginica						
	18	105	100			
	setosa	virginica	versicolor			

```
Levels: setosa versicolor virginica
```

Boosting

Unlike with bagging, where multiple copies of Bootstrap samples are created, a new model is fitted for each copy of the dataset, and all the individual models are combined to create a single predictive model, each new model is built using information from previously built models. Boosting can be understood as an iterative method involving two steps:

- A new model is built on the residuals of previous models instead of the response variable
- Now, the residuals are calculated from this model and updated to the residuals used in the previous step

The preceding two steps are repeated for multiple iterations, allowing each new model to learn from its previous mistakes, thereby improving the model accuracy:

```
#Boosting in R
library(gbm)
data(iris)
sample = iris[sample(nrow(iris)),]
train = sample[1:105,]
test = sample[106:150,]
model = gbm(Species~.,data=train,distribution="multinomial",n.
trees=5000,interaction.depth=4)
summary(model)
```

```
> summary(model)
                          var    rel.inf
Petal.Length Petal.Length 67.440852
Petal.Width   Petal.Width 24.942084
Sepal.Width   Sepal.Width  7.617065
Sepal.Length Sepal.Length  0.000000
```

The output of the preceding code is as follows:

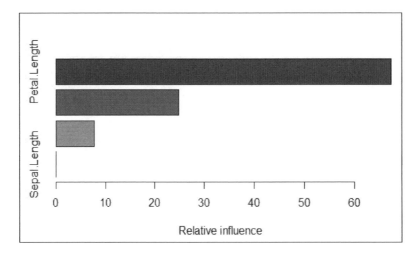

In the following code snippet, the output value for the `predict()` function is used in the `apply()` function to pick the response with the highest probability among each row in the `pred` matrix. The resultant output from the `apply()` function is the prediction for the response variable:

```
//the preceding summary states the relative importance of the
variables of the model.
```

```
pred = predict(model,newdata=test[,-5],n.trees=5000)

pred[1:5,,]
        setosa versicolor virginica
[1,]   5.630363  -2.947531 -5.172975
[2,]   5.640313  -3.533578 -5.103582
[3,]  -5.249303   3.742753 -3.374590
[4,]  -5.271020   4.047366 -3.770332
[5,]  -5.249324   3.819050 -3.439450

//pick the response with the highest probability from the resulting
pred matrix, by doing apply(.., 1, which.max) on the vector output
from prediction.
p.pred <- apply(pred,1,which.max)
p.pred
[1] 1 1 3 3 2 2 3 1 3 1 3 2 2 1 2 3 2 2 3 3 1 1 3 1 3 3 3 1 1 2 2 2 2
2 2 2 1 1 3 1 2
[42] 1 3 2 3
```

Evaluating data-mining algorithms

In the previous sections, we have seen various data-mining techniques used in recommender systems. In this section, you will learn how to evaluate models built using data-mining techniques. The ultimate goal for any data analytics model is to perform well on future data. This objective could be achieved only if we build a model that is efficient and robust during the development stage.

While evaluating any model, the most important things we need to consider are as follows:

- Whether the model is over fitting or under fitting
- How well the model fits the future data or test data

Under fitting, also known as bias, is a scenario when the model doesn't even perform well on training data. This means that we fit a less robust model to the data. For example, say the data is distributed non-linearly and we are fitting the data with a linear model. From the following image, we see that data is non-linearly distributed. Assume that we have fitted a linear model (orange line). In this case, during the model building stage itself, the predictive power will be low.

Over fitting is a scenario when the model performs well on training data, but does really bad on test data. This scenario arises when the model memorizes the data pattern rather than learning from data. For example, say the data is distributed in a non-linear pattern, and we have fitted a complex model, shown using the green line. In this case, we observe that the model is fitted very close to the data distribution, taking care of all the ups and downs. In this case, the model is most likely to fail on previously unseen data.

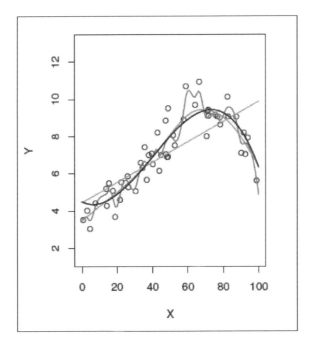

The preceding image shows simple, complex, and appropriate fitted models' training data. The green fit represents overfitting, the orange line represents underfitting, the black and blue lines represent the appropriate model, which is a trade-off between underfit and overfit.

Any fitted model is evaluated to avoid previously mentioned scenarios using cross validation, regularization, pruning, model comparisons, ROC curves, confusion matrices, and so on .

Cross validation: This is a very popular technique for model evaluation for almost all models. In this technique, we divide the data into two datasets: a training dataset and a test dataset. The model is built using the training dataset and evaluated using the test dataset. This process is repeated many times. The test errors are calculated for every iteration. The averaged test error is calculated to generalize the model accuracy at the end of all the iterations.

Regularization: In this technique, the data variables are penalized to reduce the complexity of the model with the objective to minimize the cost function. There are two most popular regularization techniques: ridge regression and lasso regression. In both techniques, we try to reduce the variable co-efficient to zero. Thus, a smaller number of variables will fit the data optimally.

Confusion matrix: This technique is popularly used in evaluating a classification model. We build a confusion matrix using the results of the model. We calculate precision and recall/sensitivity/specificity to evaluate the model.

Precision: This is the probability whether the truly classified records are relevant.

Recall/Sensitivity: This is the probability whether the relevant records are truly classified.

Specificity: Also known as true negative rate, this is the proportion of truly classified wrong records.

A confusion matrix shown in the following image is constructed using the results of classification models discussed in the previous section:

		ACTUAL	
		POSITIVE	NEGATIVE
PREDICTED	**POSITIVE**	*TRUE POSITIVE*	*FALSE POSITIVE*
	NEGATIVE	*FALSE NEGATIVE*	*TRUE NEGATIVE*

Let's understand the confusion matrix:

TRUE POSITVE (TP): This is a count of all the responses where the actual response is negative and the model predicted is positive

FALSE POSITIVE (FP): This is a count of all the responses where the actual response is negative, but the model predicted is positive. It is, in general, a **FALSE ALARM**.

FALSE NEGATIVE (FN): This is a count of all the responses where the actual response is positive, but the model predicted is negative. It is, in general, **A MISS**.

TRUE NEGATIVE (TN): This is a count of all the responses where the actual response is negative, and the model predicted is negative.

Mathematically, precision and recall/specificity is calculated as follows:

sensitivity **or true positive rate (TPR)**

$$TPR = TP/P = TP/(TP + FN)$$

specificity (SPC) or true negative rate (TNR)

$$SPC = TN/N = TN/(TN + FP)$$

precision **or positive predictive value (PPV)**

$$PPV = TP/(TP + FP)$$

Model comparison: A classification problem can be solved using one or more statistical models. For example, a classification problem can be solved using logistic regression, a decision tree, ensemble methods, and SVM. How do you choose which model fits the data well? A number of approaches are available for a suitable model selection, such as **Akaike information criteria (AIC)**, **Bayesian information criteria (BIC)**, and Adjusted R^2, C_ϱ. For each model, AIC / BIC / Adjusted R^2 is calculated. The model with least of these values is selected as the best model.

Downloading the example code

You can download the example code fies from your account at http://www.packtpub.com for all the Packt Publishing books you have purchased. If you purchased this book elsewhere, you can visit http://www.packtpub.com/support and register to have the fies e-mailed directly to you.

Summary

In this chapter, you learned about popular data preprocessing techniques, data-mining techniques, and evaluation techniques commonly used in recommender systems. In the next chapter, you will learn about the recommender systems introduced in *Chapter 1, Getting Started with Recommender Systems*, in more detail.

3

Recommender Systems

This chapter shows some popular recommendation techniques. In addition, we will implement some of them in R.

We will deal with the following techniques:

- **Collaborative filtering**: This is the branch of techniques that we will explore in detail. The algorithms are based on information about similar users or similar items. The two sub-branches are as follows:

  - **Item-based collaborative filtering**: This recommends to a user the items that are most similar to the user's purchases

  - **User-based collaborative filtering**: This recommends to a user the items that are the most preferred by similar users

- **Content-based filtering**: This is for each user; it defines a user profile and identify the items that match it.

- **Hybrid filtering**: This combines different techniques.

- **Knowledge-based filtering**: This is uses explicit knowledge about users and items.

R package for recommendation – recommenderlab

In this chapter, we will build recommender systems using `recommenderlab`, which is an R package for collaborative filtering. This section will present a quick overview of this package. First, let's install it, if we haven't done so already:

```
if(!"recommenderlab" %in% rownames(installed.packages())){
install.packages("recommenderlab")}
```

Now, we can load the package. Then, using the `help` function, we can take a look at its documentation:

```
library("recommenderlab")
help(package = "recommenderlab")
```

When we run the preceding command in RStudio, a help file containing some links and a list of functions will open.

The examples that you will see in this chapter contain some random components. In order to be able to reproduce the code obtaining the same output, we need to run this line:

```
set.seed(1)
```

We are now ready to start exploring `recommenderlab`.

Datasets

Like many other R packages, `recommenderlab` contains some datasets that can be used to play around with the functions:

```
data_package <- data(package = "recommenderlab")
data_package$results[, "Item"]
```

Jester5k, MSWeb, and MovieLense

In our examples, we will use the `MovieLense` dataset; the data is about movies. The table contains the ratings that the users give to movies. Let's load the data and take a look at it:

```
data(MovieLense)
MovieLense
## 943 x 1664 rating matrix of class 'realRatingMatrix' with
99392 ratings.
```

Each row of `MovieLense` corresponds to a user, and each column corresponds to a movie. There are more than *943 x 1664 = 1,500,000* combinations between a user and a movie. Therefore, storing the complete matrix would require more than 1,500,000 cells. However, not every user has watched every movie. Therefore, there are fewer than 100,000 ratings, and the matrix is sparse. The `recommenderlab` package allows us to store it in a compact way.

The class for rating matrices

In this section, we will explore MovieLense in detail:

```
class(MovieLense)
## [1] "realRatingMatrix"
## attr(,"package")
## [1] "recommenderlab"
```

The realRatingMatrix class is defined by recommenderlab, and ojectsojectsb contains sparse rating matrices. Let's take a look at the methods that we can apply on the objects of this class:

```
methods(class = class(MovieLense))
```

[	dimnames<-	Recommender
binarize	dissimilarity	removeKnownRatings
calcPredictionAccuracy	evaluationScheme	rowCounts
calcPredictionAccuracy	getData.frame	rowMeans
colCounts	getList	rowSds
colMeans	getNormalize	rowSums
colSds	getRatings	sample
colSums	getTopNLists	show
denormalize	image	similarity
dim	normalize	
dimnames	nratings	

Some methods that are applicable to matrices have been redefined in a more optimized way. For instance, we can use dim to extract the number of rows and columns, and colSums to compute the sum of each column. In addition, there are new methods that are specific for recommendation systems.

Usually, rating matrices are sparse matrices. For this reason, the realRatingMatrix class supports a compact storage of sparse matrices. Let's compare the size of MovieLense with the corresponding R matrix:

```
object.size(MovieLense)
## 1388448 bytes
object.size(as(MovieLense, "matrix"))
## 12740464 bytes
```

We can compute how many times the `recommenderlab` matrix is more compact:

```
object.size(as(MovieLense, "matrix")) / object.size(MovieLense)
## 9.17604692433566 bytes
```

As expected, `MovieLense` occupies much less space than the equivalent standard R matrix. The rate is about *1:9*, and the reason is the sparsity of `MovieLense`. A standard R matrix object stores all the missing values as 0s, so it stores 15 times more cells.

Computing the similarity matrix

Collaborative filtering algorithms are based on measuring the similarity between users or between items. For this purpose, `recommenderlab` contains the `similarity` function. The supported methods to compute similarities are `cosine`, `pearson`, and `jaccard`.

For instance, we might want to determine how similar the first five users are with each other. Let's compute this using the `cosine` distance:

```
similarity_users <- similarity(MovieLense[1:4, ], method =
"cosine", which = "users")
```

The `similarity_users` object contains all the dissimilarities. Let's explore it:

```
class(similarity_users)
## [1] "dist"
```

As expected, `similarity_users` is an object containing distances. Since `dist` is a base R class, we can use it in different ways. For instance, we could use `hclust` to build a hierarchic clustering model.

We can also convert `similarity_users` into a matrix and visualize it:

```
as.matrix(similarity_users)
```

1	2	3	4
0	0.1689	0.03827	0.06635
0.1689	0	0.09707	0.1531
0.03827	0.09707	0	0.3334
0.06635	0.1531	0.3334	0

Using `image`, we can visualize the matrix. Each row and each column corresponds to a user, and each cell corresponds to the similarity between two users:

```
image(as.matrix(similarity_users), main = "User similarity")
```

The more red the cell is, the more similar two users are. Note that the diagonal is red, since it's comparing each user with itself:

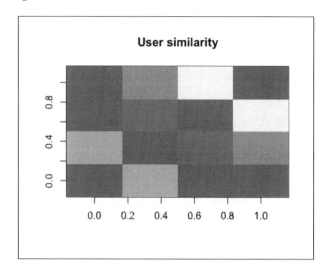

Using the same approach, we can compute and visualize the similarity between the first four items:

```
similarity_items <- similarity(MovieLense[, 1:4], method =
"cosine", which = "items")
as.matrix(similarity_items)
```

	Toy Story (1995)	GoldenEye (1995)
Toy Story (1995)	0	0.4024
GoldenEye (1995)	0.4024	0
Four Rooms (1995)	0.3302	0.2731
Get Shorty (1995)	0.4549	0.5026

The table continues as follows:

	Four Rooms (1995)	Get Shorty (1995)
Toy Story (1995)	0.3302	0.4549
GoldenEye (1995)	0.2731	0.5026
Four Rooms (1995)	0	0.3249
Get Shorty (1995)	0.3249	0

Similar to the preceding screenshot, we can visualize the matrix using this image:

```
image(as.matrix(similarity_items), main = "Item similarity")
```

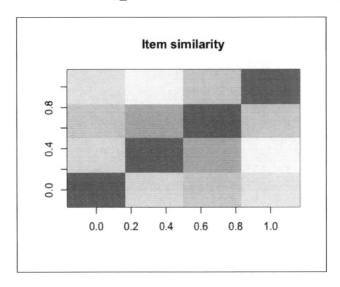

The similarity is the base of collaborative filtering models.

Recommendation models

The `recommenderlab` package contains some options for the recommendation algorithm. We can display the model applicable to the `realRatingMatrix` objects using `recommenderRegistry$get_entries`:

```
recommender_models <- recommenderRegistry$get_entries(dataType = "realRatingMatrix")
```

The `recommender_models` object contains some information about the models. First, let's see which models we have:

```
names(recommender_models)
```

Models
IBCF_realRatingMatrix
PCA_realRatingMatrix
POPULAR_realRatingMatrix
RANDOM_realRatingMatrix
SVD_realRatingMatrix
UBCF_realRatingMatrix

Let's take a look at their descriptions:

```
lapply(recommender_models, "[[", "description")
## $IBCF_realRatingMatrix
## [1] "Recommender based on item-based collaborative filtering (real
data)."
##
## $PCA_realRatingMatrix
## [1] "Recommender based on PCA approximation (real data)."
##
## $POPULAR_realRatingMatrix
## [1] "Recommender based on item popularity (real data)."
##
## $RANDOM_realRatingMatrix
## [1] "Produce random recommendations (real ratings)."
##
## $SVD_realRatingMatrix
## [1] "Recommender based on SVD approximation (real data)."
##
## $UBCF_realRatingMatrix
## [1] "Recommender based on user-based collaborative filtering (real
data)."
```

Out of them, we will use IBCF and UBCF.

The recommender_models object also contains some other information, such as its parameters:

```
recommender_models$IBCF_realRatingMatrix$parameters
```

Parameter	Default
k	30
method	Cosine
normalize	center
normalize_sim_matrix	FALSE
alpha	0.5
na_as_zero	FALSE

For a more detailed description of the package and some use cases, you can take a look at the package vignette. You can find all the material by typing help(package = "recommenderlab").

The `recommenderlab` package is a good and flexible package to perform recommendation. If we combine its models with other R tools, we will have a powerful framework to explore the data and build recommendation models.

In the next section, we will explore a dataset of `recommenderlab` using some of its tools.

Data exploration

In this section, we will explore the `MovieLense` dataset. For this purpose, we will use `recommenderlab` to build recommender systems and `ggplot2` to visualize their results. Let's load the packages and the data:

```
library("recommenderlab")
library("ggplot2")
data(MovieLense)
class(MovieLense)
## [1] "realRatingMatrix"
## attr(,"package")
## [1] "recommenderlab"
```

`MovieLense` is a `realRatingMatrix` object containing a dataset about movie ratings. Each row corresponds to a user, each column to a movie, and each value to a rating.

Exploring the nature of the data

Let's take a quick look at `MovieLense`. As explained in the previous section, there are some generic methods that can be applied to `realRatingMatrix` objects. We can extract their size using `dim`:

```
dim(MovieLense)
## [1]  943 1664
```

There are `943` users and `1664` movies. Since `realRatingMatrix` is an S4 class, the components of the objects are contained in `MovieLense` slots. We can see all the slots using `slotNames`, which displays all the data stored within an object:

```
slotNames(MovieLense)
## [1] "data"      "normalize"
MovieLense contains a data slot. Let's take a look at it.
class(MovieLense@data)
## [1] "dgCMatrix"
## attr(,"package")
## [1] "Matrix"
dim(MovieLense@data)
## [1]  943 1664
```

`MovieLense@data` belongs to the `dgCMatrix` class that inherits from `Matrix`. In order to perform custom data exploration, we might need to access this slot.

Exploring the values of the rating

Starting from the slot data, we can explore the matrix. Let's take a look at the ratings. We can convert the matrix into a vector and explore its values:

```
vector_ratings <- as.vector(MovieLense@data)
unique(vector_ratings)
## [1] 5 4 0 3 1 2
```

The ratings are integers in the range 0-5. Let's count the occurrences of each of them.

```
table_ratings <- table(vector_ratings)
table_ratings
```

Rating	Occurrences
0	1469760
1	6059
2	11307
3	27002
4	33947
5	21077

According to the documentation, a rating equal to 0 represents a missing value, so we can remove them from `vector_ratings`:

```
vector_ratings <- vector_ratings[vector_ratings != 0]
```

Now, we can build a frequency plot of the ratings. In order to visualize a bar plot with frequencies, we can use `ggplot2`. Let's convert them into categories using factor and build a quick chart:

```
vector_ratings <- factor(vector_ratings)
```

Let's visualize their distribution using `qplot`:

```
qplot(vector_ratings) + ggtitle("Distribution of the ratings")
```

The following image shows the distribution of the ratings:

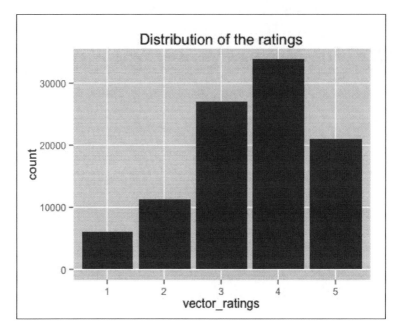

Most of the ratings are above **2**, and the most common is **4**.

Exploring which movies have been viewed

Starting with MovieLense, we can easily extract quick results using methods such as the following ones:

- colCounts: This is the number of non-missing values for each column
- colMeans: This is the average value for each column

For instance, which are the most viewed movies? We can use colCounts for this purpose. First, let's count the views for each movie:

```
views_per_movie <- colCounts(MovieLense)
```

Then, we can sort the movies by number of views:

```
table_views <- data.frame(
  movie = names(views_per_movie),
  views = views_per_movie
  )
table_views <- table_views[order(table_views$views, decreasing =
TRUE), ]
```

Now, we can visualize the first six rows and build a histogram:

```
ggplot(table_views[1:6, ], aes(x = movie, y = views)) +
geom_bar(stat="identity") + theme(axis.text.x =
element_text(angle = 45, hjust = 1)) + ggtitle("Number of views
of the top movies")
```

The following image shows the number of views of the top movies:

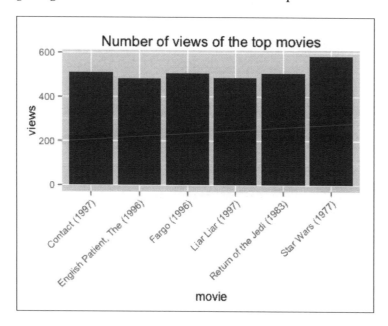

In the preceding chart, you can notice that **Star Wars (1977)** is the most viewed movie, exceeding the others by about 100 views.

Exploring the average ratings

We can identify the top-rated movies by computing the average rating of each of them. For this purpose, we can use `colMeans`; it automatically ignores the 0s, since they represent missing values. Let's take a look at the distribution of the average movie rating:

```
average_ratings <- colMeans(MovieLense)
```

Let's build the chart using `qplot`:

```
qplot(average_ratings) + stat_bin(binwidth = 0.1) +
ggtitle("Distribution of the average movie rating")
```

The following image shows the distribution of the average movie rating:

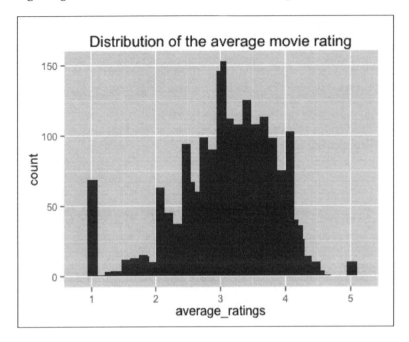

The highest value is around 3, and there are a few movies whose rating is either 1 or 5. Probably, the reason is that these movies received a rating from a few people only, so we shouldn't take them into account. We can remove the movies whose number of views is below a defined threshold, for instance, below `100`:

```
average_ratings_relevant <- average_ratings[views_per_movie > 100]
```

Let's build the chart:

```
qplot(average_ratings_relevant) + stat_bin(binwidth = 0.1) +
ggtitle(paste("Distribution of the relevant average ratings"))
```

The following image shows the distribution of the relevant average ratings:

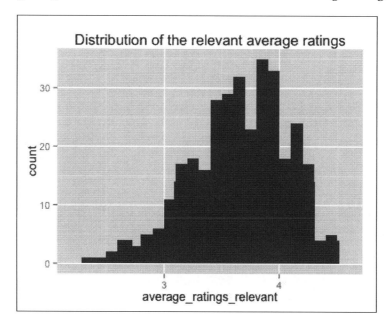

All the rankings are between 2.3 and 4.5. As expected, we removed the extremes. The highest value changes, and now, it is around 4.

Visualizing the matrix

We can visualize the matrix by building a heat map whose colors represent the ratings. Each row of the matrix corresponds to a user, each column to a movie, and each cell to its rating. For this purpose, we can use the generic method: `image`. The `recommenderlab` package redefined the method image for `realRatingMatrix` objects.

Let's build the heatmap using `image`:

```
image(MovieLense, main = "Heatmap of the rating matrix")
```

The following image displays the heatmap of the rating matrix:

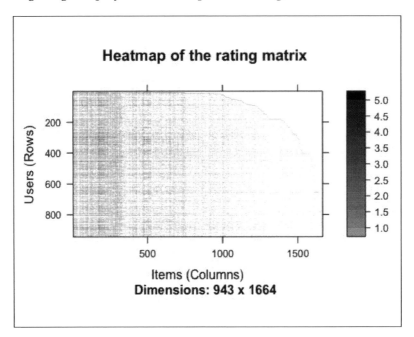

We can notice a white area in the top-right region. The reason is that the row and columns are sorted.

Since there are too many users and items, this chart is hard to read. We can build another chart zooming in on the first rows and columns.

Let's build the heat map using `image`:

```
image(MovieLense[1:10, 1:15], main = "Heatmap of the first rows and
columns")
```

The following image shows the heatmap of the first rows and columns:

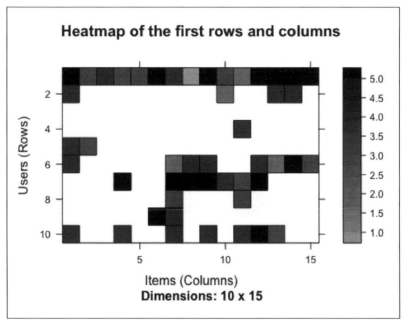

Some users saw more movies than the others. However, this chart is just displaying some random users and items. What if, instead, we select the most relevant users and items? This means visualizing only the users who have seen many movies and the movies that have been seen by many users. To identify and select the most relevant users and movies, follow these steps:

1. Determine the minimum number of movies per user.
2. Determine the minimum number of users per movie.
3. Select the users and movies matching these criteria.

For instance, we can visualize the top percentile of users and movies. In order to do this, we use the quantile function:

```
min_n_movies <- quantile(rowCounts(MovieLense), 0.99)
min_n_users <- quantile(colCounts(MovieLense), 0.99)
min_n_movies
##     99%
## 440.96
min_n_users
##     99%
## 371.07
```

Now, we can visualize the rows and columns matching the criteria.

Let's build the heat map using `image`:

```
image(MovieLense[rowCounts(MovieLense) > min_n_movies,
colCounts(MovieLense) > min_n_users], main = "Heatmap of the top users
and movies")
```

The following image displays the heatmap of the top users and movies:

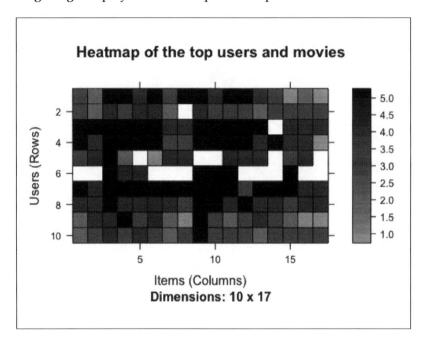

Let's take account of the users having watched more movies. Most of them have seen all the top movies, and this is not surprising. We can notice some columns that are darker than the others. These columns represent the highest-rated movies. Conversely, darker rows represent users giving higher ratings. Because of this, we might need to normalize the data.

In this section, we have explored the data. In the next section, we will process and transform it in order to have the inputs for the recommendation models.

Data preparation

This section will show you how to prepare the data to be used in recommender models. Follow these steps:

1. Select the relevant data.
2. Normalize the data.

Selecting the most relevant data

When we explored the data, we noticed that the table contains:

- Movies that have been viewed only a few times. Their ratings might be biased because of lack of data.
- Users who rated only a few movies. Their ratings might be biased.

We need to determine the minimum number of users per movie and vice versa. The correct solution comes from an iteration of the entire process of preparing the data, building a recommendation model, and validating it. Since we are implementing the model for the first time, we can use a rule of thumb. After having built the models, we can come back and modify the data preparation.

We will define `ratings_movies` containing the matrix that we will use. It takes account of:

- Users who have rated at least 50 movies
- Movies that have been watched at least 100 times

The preceding points are defined in the following code:

```
ratings_movies <- MovieLense[rowCounts(MovieLense) > 50,
colCounts(MovieLense) > 100] ratings_movies
## 560 x 332 rating matrix of class 'realRatingMatrix' with 55298
ratings.
```

The `ratings_movies` object contains about half of the users and a fifth of the movies in comparison with `MovieLense`.

Exploring the most relevant data

Using the same approach as we did in the previous section, let's visualize the top 2 percent of users and movies in the new matrix:

```
# visualize the top matrix
min_movies <- quantile(rowCounts(ratings_movies), 0.98)
min_users <- quantile(colCounts(ratings_movies), 0.98)
```

Let's build the heatmap:

```
image(ratings_movies[rowCounts(ratings_movies) > min_movies,
colCounts(ratings_movies) > min_users], main = "Heatmap of the top
users and movies")
```

The following image displays the heatmap of the top users and movies:

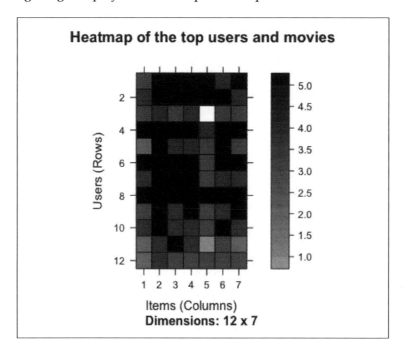

As we already noticed, some rows are darker than the others. This might mean that some users give higher ratings to all the movies. However, we have visualized the top movies only. In order to have an overview of all the users, let's take a look at the distribution of the average rating by user:

```
average_ratings_per_user <- rowMeans(ratings_movies)
```

Let's visualize the distribution:

```
qplot(average_ratings_per_user) + stat_bin(binwidth = 0.1) +
ggtitle("Distribution of the average rating per user")
```

The following image shows the distribution of the average rating per user:

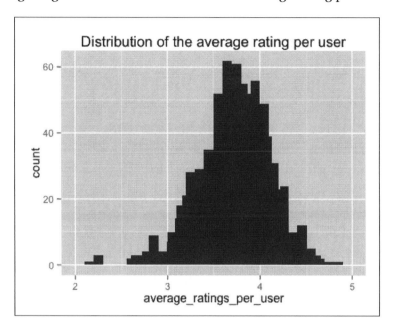

As suspected, the average rating varies a lot across different users.

Normalizing the data

Having users who give high (or low) ratings to all their movies might bias the results. We can remove this effect by normalizing the data in such a way that the average rating of each user is 0. The prebuilt `normalize` function does it automatically:

```
ratings_movies_norm <- normalize(ratings_movies)
```

Let's take a look at the average rating by users:

```
sum(rowMeans(ratings_movies_norm) > 0.00001)
## [1] 0
```

As expected, the mean rating of each user is 0 (apart from the approximation error). We can visualize the new matrix using `image`. Let's build the heat map:

```
# visualize the normalized matrix
image(ratings_movies_norm[rowCounts(ratings_movies_norm) > min_movies,
colCounts(ratings_movies_norm) > min_users], main = "Heatmap of the
top users and movies")
```

The following image shows the heatmap of the top users and movies:

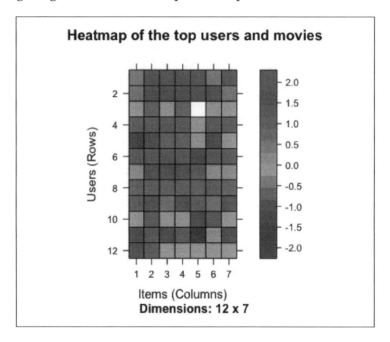

The first difference that we can notice is the colors, and this is because the data is continuous. Previously, the rating was an integer between 1 and 5. After the normalization, the rating can be any number between -5 and 5.

There are still some lines that are more blue and some that are more red. The reason is that we are visualizing only the top movies. We already checked that the average rating is 0 for each user.

Binarizing the data

Some recommendation models work on binary data, so we might want to binarize our data, that is, define a table containing only 0s and 1s. The 0s will be either treated as missing values or as bad ratings.

In our case, we can either:

- Define a matrix having 1 if the user rated the movie, and 0 otherwise. In this case, we are losing the information about the rating.
- Define a matrix having 1 if the rating is above or equal to a definite threshold (for example, 3), and 0 otherwise. In this case, giving a bad rating to a movie is equivalent to not having rated it.

Depending on the context, one choice is more appropriate than the other.

The function to binarize the data is `binarize`. Let's apply it to our data. First, let's define a matrix equal to 1 if the movie has been watched, that is if its rating is at least 1:

```
ratings_movies_watched <- binarize(ratings_movies, minRating = 1)
```

Let's take a look at the results. In this case, we will have black-and-white charts so that we can visualize a larger portion of users and movies, for example, 5 percent. Similarly, let's select this 5 percent using `quantile`. The row and column counts are the same as the original matrix, so we can still apply `rowCounts` and `colCounts` on `ratings_movies`:

```
min_movies_binary <- quantile(rowCounts(ratings_movies), 0.95)
min_users_binary <- quantile(colCounts(ratings_movies), 0.95)
```

Let's build the heat map:

```
image(ratings_movies_watched[rowCounts(ratings_movies) > min_movies_
binary,colCounts(ratings_movies) > min_users_binary], main = "Heatmap
of the top users and movies")
```

The following image shows the heat map of the top users and movies:

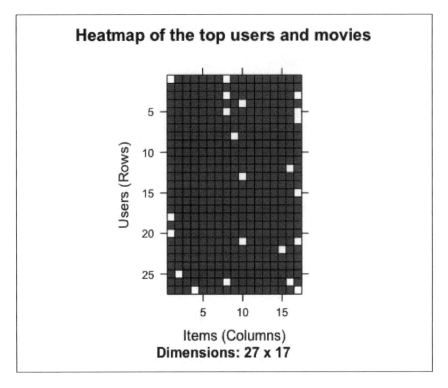

Only a few cells contain unwatched movies. This is just because we selected the top users and movies.

Let's use the same approach to compute and visualize the other binary matrix The cells having a rating above the threshold will have their value equal to 1 and the other cells will be 0s:

```
ratings_movies_good <- binarize(ratings_movies, minRating = 3)
```

Let's build the heat map:

```
image(ratings_movies_good[rowCounts(ratings_movies) > min_movies_
binary, colCounts(ratings_movies) > min_users_binary], main = "Heatmap
of the top users and movies")
```

The following image shows the heatmap of the top users and movies:

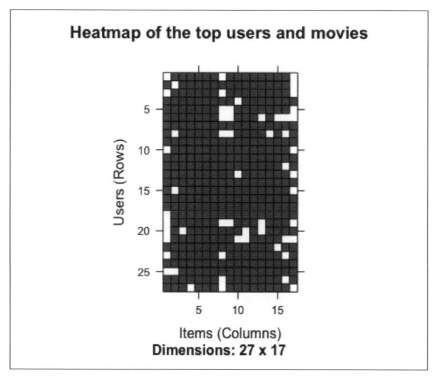

As expected, we have more white cells now. Depending on the model, we can leave the ratings matrix as it is or normalize/binarize it.

In this section, we prepared the data to perform recommendations. In the upcoming sections, we will build collaborative filtering models.

Item-based collaborative filtering

Collaborative filtering is a branch of recommendation that takes account of the information about different users. The word "collaborative" refers to the fact that users collaborate with each other to recommend items. In fact, the algorithms take account of user purchases and preferences. The starting point is a rating matrix in which rows correspond to users and columns correspond to items.

This section will show you an example of item-based collaborative filtering. Given a new user, the algorithm considers the user's purchases and recommends similar items. The core algorithm is based on these steps:

1. For each two items, measure how similar they are in terms of having received similar ratings by similar users

2. For each item, identify the *k*-most similar items

3. For each user, identify the items that are most similar to the user's purchases

In this chapter, we will see the overall approach to building an IBCF model. In addition, the upcoming sections will show its details.

Defining the training and test sets

We will build the model using a part of the MovieLense dataset (the training set) and apply it on the other part (the test set). Since it's not a topic of this chapter, we will not evaluate the model, but will only recommend movies to the users in the test set.

The two sets are as follows:

- **Training set**: This set includes users from which the model learns
- **Test set**: This set includes users to whom we recommend movies

The algorithm automatically normalizes the data, so we can use ratings_movies that contains relevant users and movies of MovieLense. We defined ratings_movies in the previous section as the subset of MovieLense users who have rated at least 50 movies and movies that have been rated at least 100 times.

First, we randomly define the which_train vector that is TRUE for users in the training set and FALSE for the others. We will set the probability in the training set as 80 percent:

```
which_train <- sample(x = c(TRUE, FALSE), size = nrow(ratings_movies),
replace = TRUE, prob = c(0.8, 0.2))
head(which_train)
## [1]  TRUE  TRUE  TRUE FALSE  TRUE FALSE
```

Let's define the training and the test sets:

```
recc_data_train <- ratings_movies[which_train, ]
recc_data_test <- ratings_movies[!which_train, ]
```

If we want to recommend items to each user, we could just use the *k*-fold:

- Split the users randomly into five groups
- Use a group as a test set and the other groups as training sets
- Repeat it for each group

This is a sample code:

```
which_set <- sample(x = 1:5, size = nrow(ratings_movies), replace =
TRUE)
for(i_model in 1:5) {
  which_train <- which_set == i_model
  recc_data_train <- ratings_movies[which_train, ]
  recc_data_test <- ratings_movies[!which_train, ]
  # build the recommender
}
```

In order to show how this package works, we split the data into training and test sets manually. You can also do this automatically in recommenderlab using the evaluationScheme function. This function also contains some tools to evaluate models that we will use in the *Chapter 4*, *Evaluating the Recommender Systems*, which is about model evaluation.

Now, we have the inputs to build and validate the model.

Building the recommendation model

The function to build models is recommender and its inputs are as follows:

- **Data**: This is the training set
- **Method**: This is the name of the technique
- **Parameters**: These are some optional parameters of the technique

The model is called IBCF, which stands for item-based collaborative filtering. Let's take a look at its parameters:

```
recommender_models <- recommenderRegistry$get_entries(dataType =
"realRatingMatrix")
recommender_models$IBCF_realRatingMatrix$parameters
```

Parameters	Default
k	30
method	Cosine
normalize	center
normalize_sim_matrix	FALSE
alpha	0.5
na_as_zero	FALSE
minRating	NA

Some relevant parameters are as follows:

- k: In the first step, the algorithm computes the similarities among each pair of items. Then, for each item, it identifies its *k* most similar items and stores it.

- method: This is the similarity function. By default, it is Cosine. Another popular option is pearson.

At the moment, we can just set them to their defaults. In order to show how to change parameters, we are setting k = 30, which is the default. We are now ready to build a recommender model:

```
recc_model <- Recommender(data = recc_data_train, method = "IBCF",
parameter = list(k = 30))
recc_model
## Recommender of type 'IBCF' for 'realRatingMatrix'
## learned using 111 users.
class(recc_model)
## [1] "Recommender"
## attr(,"package")
## [1] "recommenderlab"
```

The recc_model class is an object of the Recommender class containing the model.

Exploring the recommender model

Using `getModel`, we can extract some details about the model, such as its description and parameters:

```
model_details <- getModel(recc_model)
model_details$description
## [1] "IBCF: Reduced similarity matrix"
model_details$k
## [1] 30
```

The `model_details$sim` component contains the similarity matrix. Let's check its structure:

```
class(model_details$sim)
## [1] "dgCMatrix"
## attr(,"package")
## [1] "Matrix"
dim(model_details$sim)
## [1] 332 332
```

As expected, `model_details$sim` is a square matrix whose size is equal to the number of items. We can explore a part of it using `image`:

```
n_items_top <- 20
```

Let's build the heat map:

```
image(model_details$sim[1:n_items_top, 1:n_items_top],
main = "Heatmap of the first rows and columns")
```

The following image displays heatmap of the first rows and columns:

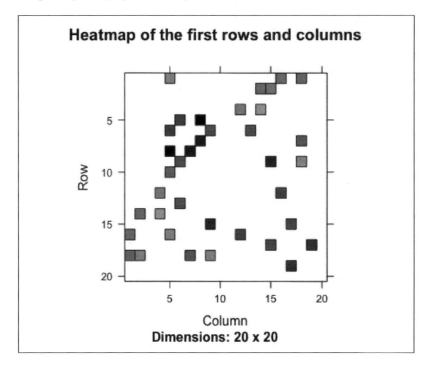

Most of the values are equal to 0. The reason is that each row contains only k elements. Let's check it:

```
model_details$k
## [1] 30
row_sums <- rowSums(model_details$sim > 0)
table(row_sums)
## row_sums
##   30
## 332
```

As expected, each row has 30 elements greater than 0. However, the matrix is not supposed to be symmetric. In fact, the number of non-null elements for each column depends on how many times the corresponding movie was included in the top k of another movie. Let's check the distribution of the number of elements by column:

```
col_sums <- colSums(model_details$sim > 0)
```

Let's build the distribution chart:

```
qplot(col_sums) + stat_bin(binwidth = 1) + ggtitle("Distribution of
the column count")
```

The following image displays the distribution of the column count:

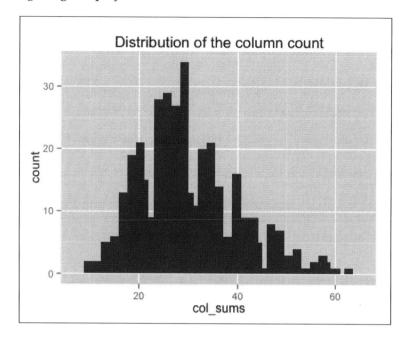

As expected, there are a few movies that are similar to many others. Let's see which are the movies with the most elements:

```
which_max <- order(col_sums, decreasing = TRUE)[1:6]
rownames(model_details$sim)[which_max]
```

Movie	col_sum
Sling Blade (1996)	62
Usual Suspects, The (1995)	60
Fargo (1996)	58
Vertigo (1958)	58
Stargate (1994)	57
The Godfather (1972)	55

Applying the recommender model on the test set

Now, we are able to recommend movies to the users in the test set. We will define n_recommended that specifies the number of items to recommend to each user. This section will show you the most popular approach to computing a weighted sum:

```
n_recommended <- 6
```

For each user, the algorithm extracts its rated movies. For each movie, it identifies all its similar items, starting from the similarity matrix. Then, the algorithm ranks each similar item in this way:

- Extract the user rating of each purchase associated with this item. The rating is used as a weight.
- Extract the similarity of the item with each purchase associated with this item.
- Multiply each weight with the related similarity.
- Sum everything up.

Then, the algorithm identifies the top *n* recommendations:

```
recc_predicted <- predict(object = recc_model, newdata = recc_data_
test, n = n_recommended)
recc_predicted
## Recommendations as 'topNList' with n = 6 for 449 users.
```

The recc_predicted object contains the recommendations. Let's take a look at its structure:

```
class(recc_predicted)
## [1] "topNList"
## attr(,"package")
## [1] "recommenderlab"
slotNames(recc_predicted)
## [1] "items"      "itemLabels" "n"
```

The slots are:

- items: This is the list with the indices of the recommended items for each user
- itemLabels: This is the name of the items
- n: This is the number of recommendations

For instance, these are the recommendations for the first user:

```
recc_predicted@items[[1]]
## [1] 201 182 254 274 193 297
```

We can extract the recommended movies from `recc_predicted@item` labels:

```
recc_user_1 <- recc_predicted@items[[1]]
movies_user_1 <- recc_predicted@itemLabels[recc_user_1]
movies_user_1
```

Index	Movie
201	Schindler's List (1993)
182	Secrets and Lies (1996)
254	Trainspotting (1996)
274	The Deer Hunter (1978)
193	L.A. Confidential (1997)
297	The Manchurian Candidate (1962)

We can define a matrix with the recommendations for each user:

```
recc_matrix <- sapply(recc_predicted@items, function(x){
  colnames(ratings_movies)[x]
})
dim(recc_matrix)
## [1]    6 449
```

Let's visualize the recommendations for the first four users:

```
recc_matrix[, 1:4]
```

Schindler's List (1993)	Babe (1995)
Secrets and Lies (1996)	The Usual Suspects (1995)
Trainspotting (1996)	Taxi Driver (1976)
The Deer Hunter (1978)	Blade Runner (1982)
L.A. Confidential (1997)	Welcome to the Dollhouse (1995)
Manchurian Candidate, The (1962)	The Silence of the Lambs (1991)
Batman Forever (1995)	Strictly Ballroom (1992)
Stargate (1994)	L.A. Confidential (1997)
Star Trek III: The Search for Spock (1984)	Cold Comfort Farm (1995)
Tin Cup (1996)	12 Angry Men (1957)
Courage Under Fire (1996)	Vertigo (1958)
Dumbo (1941)	A Room with a View (1986)

Now, we can identify the most recommended movies. For this purpose, we will define a vector with all the recommendations, and we will build a frequency plot:

```
number_of_items <- factor(table(recc_matrix))
chart_title <- "Distribution of the number of items for IBCF"
```

Let's build the distribution chart:

```
qplot(number_of_items) + ggtitle(chart_title)
```

The following image shows the distribution of the number of items for IBCF:

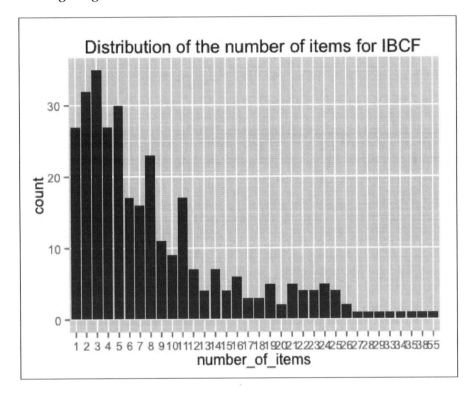

Most of the movies have been recommended only a few times, and a few movies have been recommended many times. Let's see which are the most popular movies:

```
number_of_items_sorted <- sort(number_of_items, decreasing = TRUE)
number_of_items_top <- head(number_of_items_sorted, n = 4)
table_top <- data.frame(names(number_of_items_top),
number_of_items_top)
table_top
```

	names.number_of_items_top
Mr. Smith Goes to Washington (1939)	Mr. Smith Goes to Washington (1939)
Babe (1995)	Babe (1995)
The Maltese Falcon (1941)	The Maltese Falcon (1941)
L.A. Confidential (1997)	L.A. Confidential (1997)

The preceding table continues as follows:

	number_of_items_top
Mr. Smith Goes to Washington (1939)	55
Babe (1995)	38
The Maltese Falcon (1941)	35
L.A. Confidential (1997)	34

IBCF recommends items on the basis of the similarity matrix. It's an eager-learning model, that is, once it's built, it doesn't need to access the initial data. For each item, the model stores the *k*-most similar, so the amount of information is small once the model is built. This is an advantage in the presence of lots of data.

In addition, this algorithm is efficient and scalable, so it works well with big rating matrices. Its accuracy is rather good, compared with other recommendation models.

In the next section, we will explore another branch of techniques: user-based collaborative filtering.

User-based collaborative filtering

In the previous section, the algorithm was based on items and the steps to identify recommendations were as follows:

- Identify which items are similar in terms of having been purchased by the same people
- Recommend to a new user the items that are similar to its purchases

In this section, we will use the opposite approach. First, given a new user, we will identify its similar users. Then, we will recommend the top-rated items purchased by similar users. This approach is called user-based collaborative filtering. For each new user, these are the steps:

1. Measure how similar each user is to the new one. Like IBCF, popular similarity measures are correlation and cosine.

2. Identify the most similar users. The options are:
    - Take account of the top *k* users (*k*-nearest_neighbors)
    - Take account of the users whose similarity is above a defined threshold

3. Rate the items purchased by the most similar users. The rating is the average rating among similar users and the approaches are:
    - Average rating
    - Weighted average rating, using the similarities as weights

4. Pick the top-rated items.

Like we did in the previous chapter, we will build a training and a test set. Now, we can start building the model directly.

Building the recommendation model

The R command to build the model is the same as the previous chapter. Now, the technique is called UBCF:

```
recommender_models <- recommenderRegistry$get_entries(dataType =
"realRatingMatrix")
recommender_models$UBCF_realRatingMatrix$parameters
```

Parameter	Default
method	cosine
nn	25
sample	FALSE
normalize	center
minRating	NA

Some relevant parameters are:

- method: This shows how to compute the similarity between users
- nn: This shows the number of similar users

Let's build a recommender model leaving the parameters to their defaults:

```
recc_model <- Recommender(data = recc_data_train, method = "UBCF")
recc_model
## Recommender of type 'UBCF' for 'realRatingMatrix'
## learned using 451 users.
```

Let's extract some details about the model using getModel:

```
model_details <- getModel(recc_model)
```

Let's take a look at the components of the model:

```
names(model_details)
```

Element
description
data
method
nn
sample
normalize
minRating

Apart from the description and parameters of model, model_details contains a data slot:

```
model_details$data
## 451 x 332 rating matrix of class 'realRatingMatrix' with 43846
ratings.
## Normalized using center on rows.
```

The model_details$data object contains the rating matrix. The reason is that UBCF is a lazy-learning technique, which means that it needs to access all the data to perform a prediction.

Applying the recommender model on the test set

In the same way as the IBCF, we can determine the top six recommendations for each new user:

```
n_recommended <- 6
recc_predicted <- predict(object = recc_model,
newdata = recc_data_test, n = n_recommended) recc_predicted
## Recommendations as 'topNList' with n = 6 for 109 users.
```

We can define a matrix with the recommendations to the test set users:

```
recc_matrix <- sapply(recc_predicted@items, function(x){
  colnames(ratings_movies)[x]
})
dim(recc_matrix)
## [1]    6 109
```

Let's take a look at the first four users:

```
recc_matrix[, 1:4]
```

The Usual Suspects (1995)	Lone Star (1996)
The Shawshank Redemption (1994)	This Is Spinal Tap (1984)
Contact (1997)	The Wrong Trousers (1993)
The Godfather (1972)	Hoop Dreams (1994)
Nikita (La Femme Nikita) (1990)	Mighty Aphrodite (1995)
Twelve Monkeys (1995)	Big Night (1996)
The Silence of the Lambs (1991)	The Usual Suspects (1995)
The Shawshank Redemption (1994)	The Wrong Trousers (1993)

Jaws (1975)	Monty Python and the Holy Grail (1974)
Schindler's List (1993)	GoodFellas (1990)
	The Godfather (1972)
Fargo (1996)	2001: A Space Odyssey (1968)

We can also compute how many times each movie got recommended and build the related frequency histogram:

```
number_of_items <- factor(table(recc_matrix))
chart_title <- "Distribution of the number of items for UBCF"
```

Let's build the distribution chart:

```
qplot(number_of_items) + ggtitle(chart_title)
```

The following image displays the distribution of the numbers of items for UBCF:

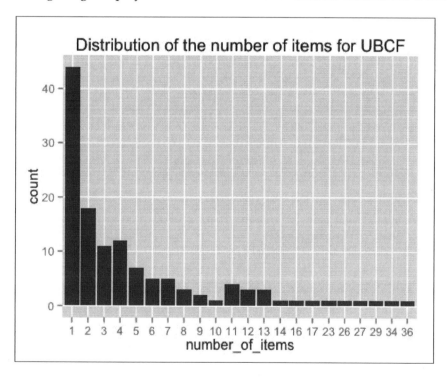

Compared with the IBCF, the distribution has a longer tail. This means that there are some movies that are recommended much more often than the others. The maximum is 29, compared with 11 for IBCF.

Let's take a look at the top titles:

```
number_of_items_sorted <- sort(number_of_items, decreasing = TRUE)
number_of_items_top <- head(number_of_items_sorted, n = 4)
table_top <- data.frame(names(number_of_items_top), number_of_items_
top)
table_top
```

	names.number_of_items_top
Schindler's List (1993)	Schindler's List (1993)
The Shawshank Redemption (1994)	The Shawshank Redemption (1994)
The Silence of the Lambs (1991)	The Silence of the Lambs (1991)
The Godfather (1972)	The Godfather (1972)

The preceding table is continued as follows:

	number_of_items_top
Schindler's List (1993)	36
The Shawshank Redemption (1994)	34
The Silence of the Lambs (1991)	29
The Godfather (1972)	27

Comparing the results of UBCF with IBCF helps in understanding the algorithm better. UBCF needs to access the initial data, so it is a lazy-learning model. Since it needs to keep the entire database in memory, it doesn't work well in the presence of a big rating matrix. Also, building the similarity matrix requires a lot of computing power and time.

However, UBCF's accuracy is proven to be slightly more accurate than IBCF, so it's a good option if the dataset is not too big.

Collaborative filtering on binary data

In the previous two sections, we built recommendation models based on user preferences, since the data displayed the rating for each purchase. However, this information is not always available. The following two scenarios can take place:

- We know which items have been purchased, but not their ratings
- For each user, we don't know which items it purchased, but we know which items it likes

In these contexts, we can build a user-item matrix whose values would be 1 if the user purchased (or liked) the item, and 0 otherwise. This case is different from the previous cases, so it should be treated separately. Similar to the other cases, the techniques are item-based and user-based.

In our case, starting from `ratings_movies`, we can build a `ratings_movies_watched` matrix whose values will be 1 if the user viewed the movie, and 0 otherwise. We built it in one of the *Binarizing the data* sections.

Data preparation

We can build `ratings_movies_watched` using the binarize method:

```
ratings_movies_watched <- binarize(ratings_movies, minRating = 1)
```

Let's take a quick look at the data. How many movies (out of 332) did each user watch? Let's build the distribution chart:

```
qplot(rowSums(ratings_movies_watched)) + stat_bin(binwidth = 10) +
geom_vline(xintercept = mean(rowSums(ratings_movies_watched)), col
= "red", linetype = "dashed") + ggtitle("Distribution of movies by
user")
```

The following image shows a distribution of movies by user:

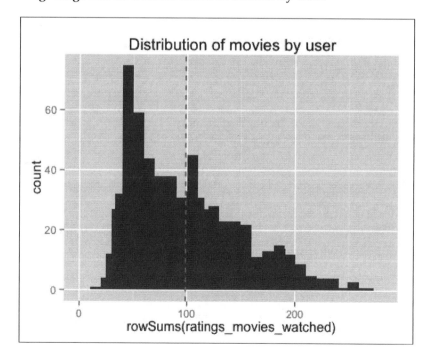

On the average, each user watched about 100 movies, and only a few watched more than 200 movies.

In order to build a recommendation model, let's define a training set and a test set:

```
which_train <- sample(x = c(TRUE, FALSE), size = nrow(ratings_movies),
replace = TRUE, prob = c(0.8, 0.2))
recc_data_train <- ratings_movies[which_train, ]
recc_data_test <- ratings_movies[!which_train, ]
```

We are now ready to build the IBCF and UBCF models.

Item-based collaborative filtering on binary data

The first step with IBCF is defining a similarity between items. In the case of binary data, distances such as the correlation and the cosine don't work properly. A good alternative is the Jaccard index. Given two items, the index is computed as the number of users purchasing both the items divided by the number of users purchasing at least one of them. Let's start from *item₁* and *item₂*, which are the sets of users purchasing the first and second item, respectively. The "∩" symbol refers to the intersection of two sets, that is, the items contained in both. The "U" symbol refers to the union of two sets, that is, the items contained in at least one of them. The Jaccard index is the number of elements in the intersection between the two sets, divided by the number of elements in their union.

$$distance(item_1, item_2) = \frac{item_1 \cap item_2}{item_1 \cup item_2}$$

We can build the IBCF filtering model using the same commands as in the previous chapters. The only difference is the input parameter method equal to `Jaccard`:

```
recc_model <- Recommender(data = recc_data_train, method = "IBCF",
parameter = list(method = "Jaccard"))
model_details <- getModel(recc_model)
```

Like in the previous sections, we can recommend six items to each of the users in the test set:

```
n_recommended <- 6
recc_predicted <- predict(object = recc_model, newdata = recc_data_
test, n = n_recommended)
recc_matrix <- sapply(recc_predicted@items, function(x){
  colnames(ratings_movies)[x]
})
```

Let's see the recommendations for the first four users.

```
recc_matrix[, 1:4]
```

L.A. Confidential (1997)	Hoop Dreams (1994)
Evita (1996)	Quiz Show (1994)
Being There (1979)	Strictly Ballroom (1992)
Chasing Amy (1997)	This Is Spinal Tap (1984)
Dr. Strangelove or: How I Learned to Stop Worrying and Love the Bomb (1963)	What's Eating Gilbert Grape (1993)
The Full Monty (1997)	The Wrong Trousers (1993)
Gone with the Wind (1939)	Cop Land (1997)
Citizen Kane (1941)	Lost Highway (1997)
On Golden Pond (1981)	Kolya (1996)
Emma (1996)	Secrets and Lies (1996)
One Flew Over the Cuckoo's Nest (1975)	Everyone Says I Love You (1996)
The Philadelphia Story (1940)	Boogie Nights (1997)

The approach is similar to IBCF using a rating matrix. Since we are not taking account of the ratings, the result will be less accurate.

User-based collaborative filtering on binary data

Similar to IBCF, we need to use the Jaccard index for UBCF. Given two users, the index is computed as the number of items purchased by both the users divided by the number of items purchased by at least one of them. The mathematical symbols are the same as in the previous section:

$$distance\left(user_1, user_2\right) = \frac{user_1 \cap user_2}{user_1 \cup user_2}$$

Let's build the recommender model:

```
recc_model <- Recommender(data = recc_data_train, method = "UBCF",
parameter = list(method = "Jaccard"))
```

Using the same commands as IBCF, let's recommend six movies to each user, and let's take a look at the first four users:

```
n_recommended <- 6
recc_predicted <- predict(object = recc_model,
newdata = recc_data_test,n = n_recommended)
recc_matrix <- sapply(recc_predicted@items, function(x){
  colnames(ratings_movies)[x]
})
dim(recc_matrix)
## [1]    6 109
recc_matrix[, 1:4]
```

The Shawshank Redemption (1994)	Titanic (1997)
Casablanca (1942)	Cinema Paradiso (1988)
Braveheart (1995)	Lone Star (1996)
The Terminator (1984)	L.A. Confidential (1997)
The Usual Suspects (1995)	Singin' in the Rain (1952)
Twelve Monkeys (1995)	Leaving Las Vegas (1995)
Titanic (1997)	Monty Python and the Holy Grail (1974)
Usual Suspects, The (1995)	The Shawshank Redemption (1994)
Groundhog Day (1993)	Schindler's List (1993)
The Shawshank Redemption (1994)	Young Frankenstein (1974)
The Blues Brothers (1980)	The Usual Suspects (1995)
Monty Python and the Holy Grail (1974)	North by Northwest (1959)

The results are different from IBCF.

These techniques assumed that the 0s are missing values. However, there is also the option to treat them as bad ratings. There is a branch of technique that deals with binary matrices only.

Most of the users don't give ratings to items, so there are several real-life cases of 0-1 matrices. That's why it's important to know how to build recommender systems in these contexts.

Conclusions about collaborative filtering

This book focuses on collaborative filtering as it's the most popular branch of recommendation. Also, it's the only one that is supported by `recommenderlab`.

However, collaborative filtering is not always the most suitable technique. This chapter provides an overview of its limitations and some alternatives.

Limitations of collaborative filtering

Collaborative filtering has some limitations. When dealing with new users and/or new items, the algorithm has these potential problems:

- If the new user hasn't seen any movie yet, neither the IBCF nor the UBCF is able to recommend any item. Unless the IBCF knows the items purchased by the new user, it can't work. The UBCF needs to know which users have similar preferences to the new one, but we don't know about its ratings.

- If the new item hasn't been purchased by anyone, it will never be recommended. IBCF matches items that have been purchased by the same users, so it won't match the new item with any of the others. UBCF recommends to each user items purchased by similar users, and no one purchased the new item. So, the algorithm won't recommend it to anyone.

Then, we might not be able to include them, and this challenge is called a cold start problem. In order to include new users and/or items, we need to take account of other information such as user profiles and item descriptions.

Another limitation of collaborative filtering is that it takes account of rating matrices only. In many contexts, we have some additional information that can improve the recommendations. In addition, user preferences are not always available, or they might be incomplete.

In the upcoming sections, we will look at some other approaches.

Content-based filtering

Another popular branch of techniques is content-based filtering. The algorithms start with a description of items, and they don't need to take account of different users at the same time. For each user, the algorithms recommend items that are similar to its past purchases.

Here are the steps to perform a recommendation:

1. Define item descriptions.
2. Define user profiles based on purchases.
3. Recommend to each user the items matching its profile

User profiles are based on their purchases, so the algorithms recommend items similar to past purchases.

Hybrid recommender systems

In many situations, we are able to build different collaborative and content-based filtering models. What if we take account of all of them at the same time? In machine learning, the approach of combining different models usually leads to better results.

A simple example is collaborative filtering combined with information about users and/or items. In the case of IBCF, the distance between items can take account of user preferences and item descriptions at the same time. Even in UBCF, the distance between users can take account of their preferences and personal data.

In the case of recommendation, these models are called hybrids. There are different ways to combine filtering models.

Parallelized hybrid systems run the recommenders separately and combine their results. There are a few options such as the following ones:

- Define a rule to pick one of the results for each user. The rule can be based on the user profile and/or on the recommendation.
- Compute an average of the rankings. The average can be weighted.

Pipelined hybrid systems run the recommenders in sequence. The output of each model is an input for the next.

Monolithic hybrid systems integrate the approaches in the same algorithm. Some options are as follows:

- **Feature combination**: This can be learned from different types of inputs. For example, an algorithm can take account of ratings, user profiles, and item descriptions.
- **Feature augmentation**: This builds the input of a recommender by combining different data sources.

Knowledge-based recommender systems

There are situations where collaborative and content-based filtering don't work.

In these contexts, we can use explicit knowledge about users and products, and recommendation criteria. This branch of techniques is called knowledge-based. There are a variety of techniques, and they depend on the data and on the business problem. For this reason, it's hard to define some techniques that are applicable in different contexts.

Summary

Among the different techniques for recommendation, collaborative filtering is the easiest to implement. In addition, content-based filtering algorithms depend on the context, and it's still possible to build them in R.

This chapter showed you different approaches to recommendation by focusing on collaborative filtering. The next chapter will show you how to test and evaluate the recommendation techniques.

4
Evaluating the Recommender Systems

The previous chapter showed you how to build recommender systems. There are a few options, and some of them can be developed using the `recommenderlab` package. In addition, each technique has some parameters. After we build the models, how can we decide which one to use? How can we determine its parameters? We can first test the performance of some models and/or parameter configurations and then choose the one that performs best.

This chapter will show you how to evaluate recommender models, compare their performances, and choose the most appropriate model. In this chapter, we will cover the following topics:

- Preparing the data to evaluate performance
- Evaluating the performance of some models
- Choosing the best performing models
- Optimizing model parameters

Preparing the data to evaluate the models

To evaluate models, you need to build them with some data and test them on some other data. This chapter will show you how to prepare the two sets of data. The `recommenderlab` package contains prebuilt tools that help in this task.

The target is to define two datasets, which are as follows:

- **Training set**: These are the models from which users learn
- **Testing set**: These are the models that users apply and test

In order to evaluate the models, we need to compare the recommendations with the user preferences. In order to do so, we need to forget about some user preferences in the test set and see whether the techniques are able to identify them. For each user in the test set, we ignore some purchases and build the recommendations based on the others. Let's load the packages:

```
library(recommenderlab)
library(ggplot2)
```

The data-set that we will use is called `MovieLense`. Let's define `ratings_movies` containing only the most relevant users and movies:

```
data(MovieLense)
ratings_movies <- MovieLense[rowCounts(MovieLense) > 50,
colCounts(MovieLense) > 100]
ratings_movies
## 560 x 332 rating matrix of class 'realRatingMatrix' with 55298
ratings.
```

We are now ready to prepare the data.

Splitting the data

The easiest way to build a training and test set is to split the data in two parts. First, we need to decide how many users to put into each part. For instance, we can put 80 percent of the users into the training set. We can define `percentage_training` by specifying the percentage of the training set:

```
percentage_training <- 0.8
```

For each user in the test set, we need to define how many items to use to generate recommendations. The remaining items will be used to test the model accuracy. It's better that this parameter is lower than the minimum number of items purchased by any user so that we don't have users without items to test the models:

```
min(rowCounts(ratings_movies))
## _18_
```

For instance, we can keep 15 items:

```
items_to_keep <- 15
```

Evaluating a model consists of comparing the recommendations with the unknown purchases. The ratings are between 1 and 5, and we need to define what constitutes good and bad items. For this purpose, we will define a threshold with the minimum rating that is considered good:

```
rating_threshold <- 3
```

There is an additional parameter defining how many times we want to run the evaluation. For the moment, let's set it to 1:

```
n_eval <- 1
```

We are ready to split the data. The `recommenderlab` function is `evaluationScheme` and its parameters are as follows:

- `data`: This is the initial dataset
- `method`: This is the way to split the data. In this case, it's `split`
- `train`: This is the percentage of data in the training set
- `given`: This is the number of items to keep
- `goodRating`: This is the rating threshold
- `k`: This is the number of times to run the evaluation

Let's build `eval_sets` containing the sets:

```
eval_sets <- evaluationScheme(data = ratings_movies, method = "split",
train = percentage_training, given = items_to_keep, goodRating =
rating_threshold, k = n_eval) eval_sets
## Evaluation scheme with 15 items given
## Method: 'split' with 1 run(s).
## Training set proportion: 0.800
## Good ratings: >=3.000000
## Data set: 560 x 332 rating matrix of class 'realRatingMatrix' with
55298 ratings.
```

In order to extract the sets, we need to use `getData`. There are three sets:

- `train`: This is the training set
- `known`: This is the test set, with the item used to build the recommendations
- `unknown`: This is the test set, with the item used to test the recommendations

Let's take a look at the training set:

```
getData(eval_sets, "train")
## 448 x 332 rating matrix of class 'realRatingMatrix' with 44472
ratings.
```

It's a `realRatingMatrix` object, so we can apply methods such as `nrow` and `rowCounts` to it:

```
nrow(getData(eval_sets, "train")) / nrow(ratings_movies)
## _0.8_
```

As expected, about 80 percent of the users are in the training set. Let's take a look at the two test sets:

```
getData(eval_sets, "known")
## 112 x 332 rating matrix of class 'realRatingMatrix' with 1680
ratings.
getData(eval_sets, "unknown")
## 112 x 332 rating matrix of class 'realRatingMatrix' with 9146
ratings.
```

They both have the same number of users. There should be about 20 percent of data in the test set:

```
nrow(getData(eval_sets, "known")) / nrow(ratings_movies)
## _0.2_
```

Everything is as expected. Let's see how many items we have for each user in the known set. It should be equal to `items_to_keep`, that is, 15:

```
unique(rowCounts(getData(eval_sets, "known")))
## _15_
```

The same is not true for the users in the test set, since the number of remaining items depends on the initial number of purchases:

```
qplot(rowCounts(getData(eval_sets, "unknown"))) + geom_
histogram(binwidth = 10) + ggtitle("unknown items by the users")
```

The following image displays the unknown items by the users:

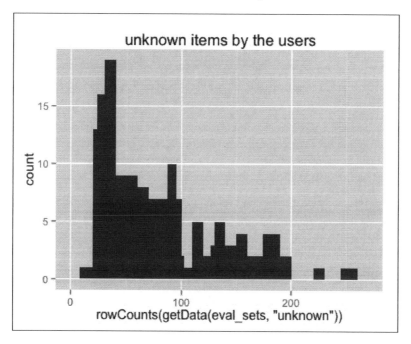

As expected, the number of items by users varies a lot.

Bootstrapping data

In the previous subsection, we split the data into two parts, and the training set contained 80 percent of the rows. What if, instead, we sample the rows with replacement? The same user can be sampled more than once and, if the training set has the same size as it did earlier, there will be more users in the test set. This approach is called bootstrapping, and it's supported by recommenderlab. The parameters are the same as the previous approach. The only difference is that we specify method = "bootstrap" instead of method = "split":

```
percentage_training <- 0.8
items_to_keep <- 15
rating_threshold <- 3
n_eval <- 1
eval_sets <- evaluationScheme(data = ratings_movies, method =
"bootstrap", train = percentage_training, given = items_to_keep,
goodRating = rating_threshold, k = n_eval)
```

The number of users in the training set is still equal to 80 percent of the total:

```
nrow(getData(eval_sets, "train")) / nrow(ratings_movies)
## _0.8_
```

However, the same is not true for the items in the test set:

```
perc_test <- nrow(getData(eval_sets, "known")) / nrow(ratings_movies)
perc_test
## _0.4393_
```

The test set is more than twice as big as the previous set.

We can extract the unique users in the training set:

```
length(unique(eval_sets@runsTrain[[1]]))
## _314_
```

The percentage of unique users in the training set should be complementary to the percentage of users in the test set, which is shown as follows:

```
perc_train <- length(unique(eval_sets@runsTrain[[1]])) / nrow(ratings_movies)
perc_train + perc_test
## _1_
```

We can count how many times each user is repeated in the training set:

```
table_train <- table(eval_sets@runsTrain[[1]])
n_repetitions <- factor(as.vector(table_train))
qplot(n_repetitions) + ggtitle("Number of repetitions in the training set")
```

The following image displays the number of repetitions in the training set:

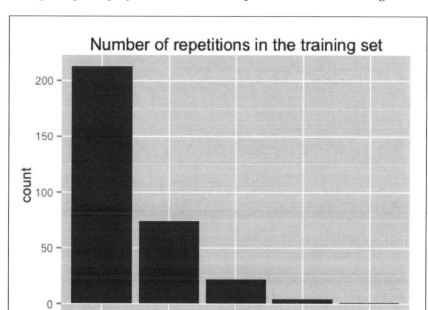

Most of the users have been sampled fewer than four times.

Using k-fold to validate models

The two previous approaches tested the recommender on part of the users. If, instead, we test the recommendation on each user, we could measure the performances much more accurately. We can split the data into some chunks, take a chunk out as the test set, and evaluate the accuracy. Then, we can do the same with each other chunk and compute the average accuracy. This approach is called k-fold and it's supported by recommenderlab.

We can use evaluationScheme and the difference is that, instead of specifying the percentage of data to put in the training set, we will define how many chunks we want. The argument is *k*, like the number of repetitions in the previous examples. Clearly, we don't need to specify train anymore:

```
n_fold <- 4
eval_sets <- evaluationScheme(data = ratings_movies, method = "cross-
validation", k = n_fold, given = items_to_keep, goodRating = rating_
threshold)
```

We can count how many items we have in each set:

```
size_sets <- sapply(eval_sets@runsTrain, length)
size_sets
## _420_, _420_, _420_ and _420_
```

As expected, all the sets have the same size.

This approach is the most accurate one, although it's computationally heavier.

In this chapter, we've seen different approaches to prepare the training and the test set. In the next chapter, we will start with the evaluation.

Evaluating recommender techniques

This chapter will show you two popular approaches to evaluate recommendations. They are both based on the cross-validation framework described in the previous section.

The first approach is to evaluate the ratings estimated by the algorithm. The other approach is to evaluate the recommendations directly. There is a subsection for each approach.

Evaluating the ratings

In order to recommend items to new users, collaborative filtering estimates the ratings of items that are not yet purchased. Then, it recommends the top-rated items. At the moment, let's forget about the last step. We can evaluate the model by comparing the estimated ratings with the real ones.

First, let's prepare the data for validation, as shown in the previous section. Since the k-fold is the most accurate approach, we will use it here:

```
n_fold <- 4
items_to_keep <- 15
rating_threshold <- 3
eval_sets <- evaluationScheme(data = ratings_movies, method = "cross-
validation", k = n_fold, given = items_to_keep, goodRating = rating_
threshold)
```

We need to define the model to evaluate. For instance, we can evaluate an item-based collaborative filtering recommender. Let's build it using the Recommender function. We need to specify the name of the model and the list of its parameters. If we use their defaults, then it's NULL:

```
model_to_evaluate <- "IBCF"
model_parameters <- NULL
```

We are now ready to build the model, using the following code:

```
eval_recommender <- Recommender(data = getData(eval_sets, "train"),
method = model_to_evaluate, parameter = model_parameters)
```

The IBCF can recommend new items and predict their ratings. In order to build the model, we need to specify how many items we want to recommend, for example, 10, even if we don't need to use this parameter in the evaluation:

```
items_to_recommend <- 10
```

We can build the matrix with the predicted ratings using the `predict` function:

```
eval_prediction <- predict(object = eval_recommender, newdata =
getData(eval_sets, "known"), n = items_to_recommend, type = "ratings")
class(eval_prediction)
## realRatingMatrix
```

The `eval_prediction` object is a rating matrix. Let's see how many movies we are recommending to each user. For this purpose, we can visualize the distribution of the number of movies per user:

```
qplot(rowCounts(eval_prediction)) + geom_histogram(binwidth = 10) +
ggtitle("Distribution of movies per user")
```

The following image displays the distribution of movies per user:

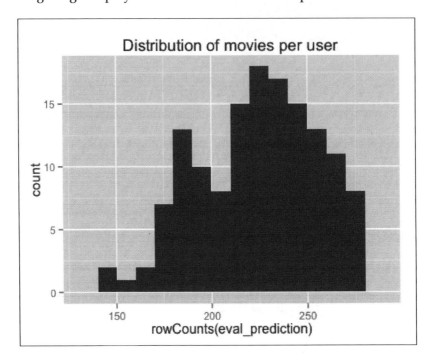

The number of movies per user is roughly between 150 and 300.

The function to measure the accuracy is `calcPredictionAccuracy` and it computes the following aspects:

- **Root mean square error (RMSE)**: This is the standard deviation of the difference between the real and predicted ratings.

- **Mean squared error (MSE)**: This is the mean of the squared difference between the real and predicted ratings. It's the square of RMSE, so it contains the same information.

- **Mean absolute error (MAE)**: This is the mean of the absolute difference between the real and predicted ratings.

We can compute these measures about each user by specifying `byUser = TRUE`:

```
eval_accuracy <- calcPredictionAccuracy(
  x = eval_prediction, data = getData(eval_sets, "unknown"), byUser =
TRUE)
head(eval_accuracy)
```

	RMSE	MSE	MAE
1	1.217	1.481	0.8205
2	0.908	0.8244	0.727
6	1.172	1.374	0.903
14	1.405	1.973	1.027
15	1.601	2.562	1.243
18	0.8787	0.7721	0.633

Let's take a look at the RMSE by a user:

```
qplot(eval_accuracy[, "RMSE"]) + geom_histogram(binwidth = 0.1) +
ggtitle("Distribution of the RMSE by user")
```

The following image displays the distribution of the RSME by user:

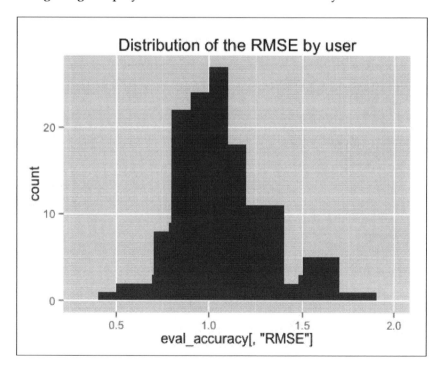

Most of the RMSEs are in the range of 0.8 to 1.4. We evaluated the model for each user. In order to have a performance index of the whole model, we need to compute the average indices, specifying byUser = FALSE:

```
eval_accuracy <- calcPredictionAccuracy(
  x = eval_prediction, data = getData(eval_sets, "unknown"), byUser =
FALSE) eval_accuracy
## _1.101_, _1.211_ and _0.8124_
```

These measures are useful to compare the performance of different models on the same data.

Evaluating the recommendations

Another way to measure accuracies is by comparing the recommendations with the purchases having a positive rating. For this purpose, we can use the prebuilt evaluate function. Its inputs are as follows:

- x: This is the object containing the evaluation scheme.

- method: This is the recommendation technique.

- n: This is the number of items to recommend to each user. If we can specify a vector of n, the function will evaluate the recommender performance depending on n.

We have already defined a threshold, rating_threshold <- 3, for positive ratings, and this parameter is already stored inside eval_sets. The progress = FALSE argument suppresses a progress report:

```
results <- evaluate(x = eval_sets, method = model_to_evaluate, n =
seq(10, 100, 10))
class(results)
## evaluationResults
```

The results object is an evaluationResults object containing the results of the evaluation. Using getConfusionMatrix, we can extract a list of confusion matrices. Each element of the list corresponds to a different split of the *k*-fold. Let's take a look at the first element:

```
head(getConfusionMatrix(results)[[1]])
```

	TP	FP	FN	TN	precision	recall	TPR	FPR
10	3.443	6.557	70.61	236.4	0.3443	0.04642	0.04642	0.02625
20	6.686	13.31	67.36	229.6	0.3343	0.09175	0.09175	0.05363
30	10.02	19.98	64.03	223	0.334	0.1393	0.1393	0.08075

	TP	FP	FN	TN	precision	recall	TPR	FPR
40	13.29	26.71	60.76	216.2	0.3323	0.1849	0.1849	0.1081
50	16.43	33.57	57.62	209.4	0.3286	0.2308	0.2308	0.1362
60	19.61	40.39	54.44	202.6	0.3268	0.2759	0.2759	0.164

The first four columns contain the true-false positives/negatives, and they are as follows:

- **True Positives (TP)**: These are recommended items that have been purchased
- **False Positives (FP)**: These are recommended items that haven't been purchased
- **False Negatives(FN)**: These are not recommended items that have been purchased
- **True Negatives (TN)**: These are not recommended items that haven't been purchased

A perfect (or overfitted) model would have only TP and TN.

If we want to take account of all the splits at the same time, we can just sum up the indices:

```
columns_to_sum <- c("TP", "FP", "FN", "TN")
indices_summed <- Reduce("+", getConfusionMatrix(results))[, columns_
to_sum]
head(indices_summed)
```

	TP	**FP**	**FN**	**TN**
10	13.05	26.95	279.3	948.7
20	25.4	54.6	267	921
30	37.74	82.26	254.7	893.4
40	50.58	109.4	241.8	866.2
50	62.35	137.7	230	838
60	74.88	165.1	217.5	810.5

Note that we could have used `avg(results)` instead.

The other four columns contain performance indices, and it's harder to summarize them across all the folds. However, we can visualize them by building some charts.

First, let's build the ROC curve. It displays these factors:

- **True Positive Rate (TPR)**: This is the percentage of purchased items that have been recommended. It's the number of TP divided by the number of purchased items (TP + FN).

- **False Positive Rate (FPR)**: This is the percentage of not purchased items that have been recommended. It's the number of FP divided by the number of not purchased items (FP + TN).

The `plot` method will build a chart with the `ROC` curve. In order to visualize the labels, we add the `annotate = TRUE` input:

```
plot(results, annotate = TRUE, main = "ROC curve")
```

The following image displays the ROC curve:

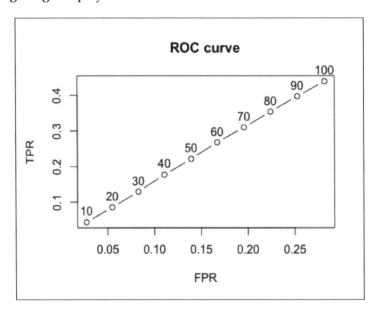

Two accuracy metrics are as follows:

- **Precision**: This is the percentage of recommended items that have been purchased. It's the number of FP divided by the total number of positives (TP + FP).

- **Recall**: This is the percentage of purchased items that have been recommended. It's the number of TP divided by the total number of purchases (TP + FN). It's also equal to the True Positive Rate.

If a small percentage of purchased items are recommended, the precision usually decreases. On the other hand, a higher percentage of purchased items will be recommended so that the recall increases:

```
plot(results, "prec/rec", annotate = TRUE, main = "Precision-recall")
```

The following image displays the precision-recall:

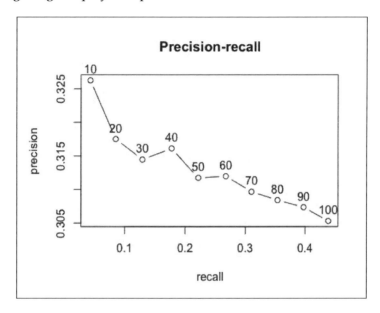

This chart reflects the tradeoff between precision and recall. Even if the curve is not perfectly monotonic, the trends are as expected.

In this section, we've seen how to evaluate a model. In the next section, we will see how to compare two or more models.

Identifying the most suitable model

The previous chapter showed you how to evaluate a model. The performance indices are useful to compare different models and/or parameters. Applying different techniques on the same data, we can compare a performance index to pick the most appropriate recommender. Since there are different evaluation metrics, there is no objective way to do it.

The starting point is the k-fold evaluation framework that we defined in the previous section. It is stored inside `eval_sets`.

Comparing models

In order to compare different models, we first need to define them. Each model is stored in a list with its name and parameters. The components of the list are as follows:

- `name`: This is the model name.
- `param`: This is a list with its parameters. It can be NULL, if all the parameters are left at their defaults.

For instance, that's how we can define an item-based collaborative filtering by setting the k parameter to `20`:

```
list(name = "IBCF", param = list(k = 20))
```

In order to evaluate different models, we can define a list with them. We can build the following filtering:

- Item-based collaborative filtering, using the Cosine as the distance function
- Item-based collaborative filtering, using the Pearson correlation as the distance function
- User-based collaborative filtering, using the Cosine as the distance function
- User-based collaborative filtering, using the Pearson correlation as the distance function
- Random recommendations to have a base line

The preceding points are defined in the following code:

```
models_to_evaluate <- list(
  IBCF_cos = list(name = "IBCF", param = list(method =
  "cosine")),
  IBCF_cor = list(name = "IBCF", param = list(method =
  "pearson")),
  UBCF_cos = list(name = "UBCF", param = list(method =
  "cosine")),
  UBCF_cor = list(name = "UBCF", param = list(method =
  "pearson")),
  random = list(name = "RANDOM", param=NULL)
)
```

In order to evaluate the models properly, we need to test them, varying the number of items. For instance, we might want to recommend up to 100 movies to each user. Since 100 is already a big number of recommendations, we don't need to include higher values:

```
n_recommendations <- c(1, 5, seq(10, 100, 10))
```

We are ready to run and evaluate the models. Like in the previous chapter, the function is `evaluate`. The only difference is that now the input method is a list of models:

```
list_results <- evaluate(x = eval_sets, method = models_to_evaluate, n
= n_recommendations)
class(list_results)
## evaluationResultList
```

The `list_results` object is an `evaluationResultList` object and it can be treated as a list. Let's take a look at its first element:

```
class(list_results[[1]])
## evaluationResults
```

The first element of `list_results` is an `evaluationResults` object, and this object is the same as the output of evaluate with a single model. We can check whether the same is true for all its elements:

```
sapply(list_results, class) == "evaluationResults"
## TRUE TRUE TRUE TRUE TRUE
```

Each element of `list_results` is an `evaluationResults` object. We can extract the related average confusion matrices using `avg`:

```
avg_matrices <- lapply(list_results, avg)
```

We can use `avg_matrices` to explore the performance evaluation. For instance, let's take a look at the IBCF with Cosine distance:

```
head(avg_matrices$IBCF_cos[, 5:8])
```

	precision	recall	TPR	FPR
1	0.3589	0.004883	0.004883	0.002546
5	0.3371	0.02211	0.02211	0.01318
10	0.3262	0.0436	0.0436	0.02692
20	0.3175	0.08552	0.08552	0.0548
30	0.3145	0.1296	0.1296	0.08277
40	0.3161	0.1773	0.1773	0.1103

We have all the metrics of the previous chapter. In the next section, we will explore these metrics to identify the best performing model.

Identifying the most suitable model

We can compare the models by building a chart displaying their ROC curves. Like the previous section, we can use `plot`. The annotate argument specifies which curves will contain the labels. For instance, the first and second curves are labeled by defining `annotate = c(1, 2)`. In our case, we will label only the first curve:

```
plot(list_results, annotate = 1, legend = "topleft") title("ROC
curve")
```

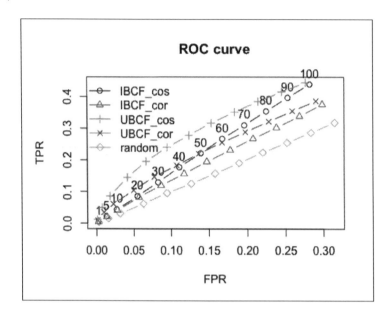

A good performance index is the **area under the curve (AUC)**, that is, the area under the ROC curve. Even without computing it, we can notice that the highest is UBCF with cosine distance, so it's the best-performing technique.

Like we did in the previous section, we can build the precision-recall chart:

```
plot(list_results, "prec/rec", annotate = 1, legend = "bottomright")
title("Precision-recall")
```

The following image shows the precision-recall:

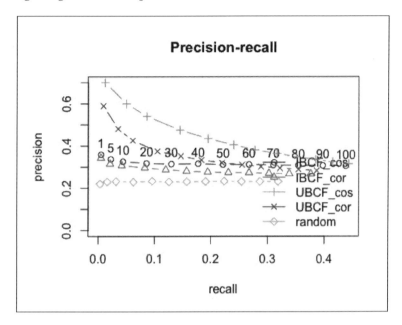

The UBCF with cosine distance is still the top model. Depending on what we want to achieve, we can set an appropriate number of items to recommend.

Optimizing a numeric parameter

Recommendation models often contain some numeric parameters. For instance, IBCF takes account of the *k*-closest items. How can we optimize *k*?

In a similar way to categoric parameters, we can test different values of a numeric parameter. In this case, we also need to define which values we want to test.

So far, we left *k* to its default value: 30. Now, we can explore more values, ranging between 5 and 40:

```
vector_k <- c(5, 10, 20, 30, 40)
```

Using `lapply`, we can define a list of models to evaluate. The distance metric is the cosine:

```
models_to_evaluate <- lapply(vector_k, function(k){
  list(name = "IBCF", param = list(method = "cosine", k = k))
})
names(models_to_evaluate) <- paste0("IBCF_k_", vector_k)
```

Using the same commands as we did earlier, let's build and evaluate the models:

```
n_recommendations <- c(1, 5, seq(10, 100, 10))
list_results <- evaluate(x = eval_sets, method = models_to_evaluate, n
= n_recommendations)
```

Building a chart with the ROC curve, we should be able to identify the best-performing *k*:

```
plot(list_results, annotate = 1,        legend = "topleft") title("ROC
curve")
```

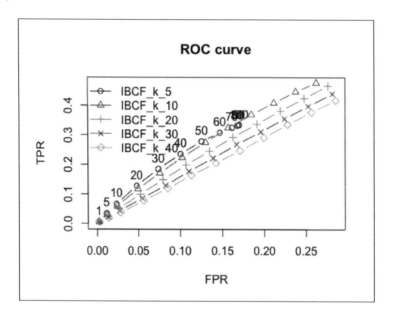

The *k* having the biggest AUC is 10. Another good candidate is 5, but it can never have a high TPR. This means that, even if we set a very high n value, the algorithm won't be able to recommend a big percentage of items that the user liked. The IBCF with k = 5 recommends only a few items similar to the purchases. Therefore, it can't be used to recommend many items.

Let's take a look at the precision-recall chart:

```
plot(list_results, "prec/rec", annotate = 1, legend = "bottomright")
title("Precision-recall")
```

The following image displays the precision-recall:

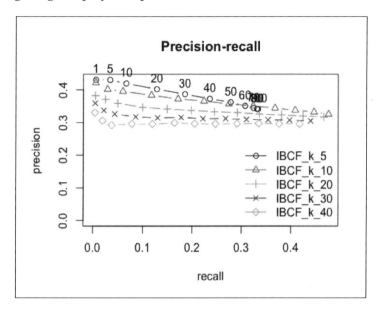

To achieve the highest recall, we need to set `k = 10`. If we are more interested in the precision, we set `k = 5`.

This section evaluated four techniques using different methods. Then, it optimized a numeric parameter of one of them. Depending on what we want to achieve, the choice of parameters might be slightly different.

Summary

This chapter showed you how to evaluate the performance of different models in order to choose the most accurate one. There are different ways to evaluate performances that might potentially lead to different choices. Depending on the business target, the evaluation metric is different. This is an example of how business and data should be combined to achieve the final result.

The next chapter will explain a complete use case in which we will prepare the data, build different models, and test them.

Case Study – Building Your Own Recommendation Engine

5

The previous two chapters showed how you how to build, test, and optimize recommender systems using R. Although the chapters were full of examples, they were based on datasets provided by an R package. The data was structured using redyal and was ready to be processed. However, in real life, the data preparation is an important, time-consuming, and tough step.

Another limitation of the previous examples is that they are based on the ratings only. In most of the situations, there are other data sources such as item descriptions and user profiles. A good solution comes from a combination of all the relevant information.

This chapter shows a practical example in which we will build and optimize a recommender system, starting from raw data. This chapter will cover the following topics:

- Preparing the data to build a recommendation engine
- Exploring the data through visualization techniques
- Choosing and building a recommendation model
- Optimizing the performance of the recommendation model by setting its parameters

In the end, we will build an engine that generates recommendations.

Preparing the data

Starting from raw data, this section will show you how to prepare the input for the recommendation models.

Description of the data

The data is about Microsoft users visiting a website during one week. For each user, the data displays which areas the users visited. For the sake of simplicity, from now on we will refer to the website areas with the term "items".

There are 5,000 users and they are represented by sequential numbers between 10,001 and 15,000. Items are represented by numbers between 1,000 and 1,297, even if they are less than 298.

The dataset is an unstructured text file. Each record contains a number of fields between 2 and 6. The first field is a letter defining what the record contains. There are three main types of records, which are as follows:

- **Attribute (A)**: This is the description of the website area
- **Case (C)**: This is the case for each user, containing its ID
- **Vote (V)**: This is the vote lines for the case

Each case record is followed by one or more votes, and there is just one case for each user.

Our target is to recommend each user to explore some areas of the website that they haven't explored yet.

Importing the data

This section will show you how to import data. First, let's load the packages that we will use:

```
library("data.table")
library("ggplot2")
library("recommenderlab")
library("countrycode")
```

The preceding code is explained in the following points:

- `data.table`: This manipulates the data
- `ggplot2`: This builds charts

- `recommenderlab`: This builds recommendation engines
- `countrycode`: This package contains the country names

Then, let's load the table into memory. If the text file is already in our working directory, it's enough to define its name. Otherwise, we need to define its full path:

```
file_in <- "anonymous-msweb.test.txt"
```

The rows contain different numbers of columns, which means that the data is unstructured. However, there are at most six columns, so we can load the file into a table using `read.csv`. The rows with fewer than six fields will have just empty values:

```
table_in <- read.csv(file_in, header = FALSE)
head(table_in)
```

V1	V2	V3	V4	V5	V6
I	4	www.microsoft.com	created by getlog.pl		
T	1	VRoot	0	0	VRoot
N	0	0			
N	1	1			
T	2	Hide1	0	0	Hide
N	0	0			

The first two columns contain the user IDs and their purchases. We can just drop the other columns:

```
table_users <- table_in[, 1:2]
```

In order to process the data more easily, we can convert it into a data table, using this command:

```
table_users <- data.table(table_users)
```

The columns are as follows:

- `category`: This is a letter specifying the content of the column. The columns containing a user or an item ID belong to the categories C and V, respectively.
- `value`: This is a number specifying the user or item ID.

We can assign the column names and select the rows containing either users or items:

```
setnames(table_users, 1:2, c("category", "value"))
table_users <- table_users[category %in% c("C", "V")]
head(table_users)
```

category	value
C	10001
V	1038
V	1026
V	1034
C	10002
V	1008

The `table_users` object contains structured data, which is our starting point to define a rating matrix.

Defining a rating matrix

Our target is to define a table having a row for each item and a column for each purchase. For each user, `table_users` contains its ID and purchases in separate rows. In each block or rows, the first column contains the user ID and the other contains the item IDs.

You can use the following steps to define a rating matrix:

1. Label the cases.
2. Define a table in the long format.
3. Define a table in the wide format.
4. Define the rating matrix.

In order to reshape the table, the first step is to define a field called `chunk_user` containing an incremental number for each user. The `category == "C"` condition is true for the user rows, which are the first rows of the chunks. Using `cumsum`, we are incrementing the index of 1 whenever there is a row with a new user:

```
table_users[, chunk_user := cumsum(category == "C")]
head(table_users)
```

category	value	chunk_user
C	10001	1
V	1038	1
V	1026	1
V	1034	1
C	10002	2
V	1008	2

The next step is to define a table in which rows correspond to the purchases. We need a column with the user ID and a column with the item ID. The new table is called `table_long`, because it's in a `long` format:

```
table_long <- table_users[, list(user = value[1], item = value[-1]), by = "chunk_user"]
head(table_long)
```

chunk_user	user	item
1	10001	1038
1	10001	1026
1	10001	1034
2	10002	1008
2	10002	1056
2	10002	1032

Now, we can define a table having a row for each user and a column for each item. The values are equal to 1 if the item has been purchased, and 0 otherwise. We can build the table using the `reshape` function. Its inputs are as follows:

- `data`: This is the table in the `long` format.
- `direction`: This shows whether we are reshaping from long to wide or otherwise.
- `idvar`: This is the variable identifying the group, which, in this case, is the user.
- `timevar`: This is the variable identifying the record within the same group. In this case, it's the item.
- `v.names`: This is name of the values. In this case, it's the rating that is always equal to one. Missing user-item combinations will be NA values.

After defining the column `value` equal to `1`, we can build `table_wide` using `reshape`:

```
table_long[, value := 1]
table_wide <- reshape(data = table_long,
                      direction = "wide",
                      idvar = "user",
                      timevar = "item",
                      v.names = "value")
head(table_wide[, 1:5, with = FALSE])
```

chunk_user	user	value.1038	value.1026	value.1034
1	10001	1	1	1
2	10002	NA	NA	NA
3	10003	1	1	NA
4	10004	NA	NA	NA
5	10005	1	1	1
6	10006	NA	NA	1

In order to build the rating matrix, we need to keep only the columns containing ratings. In addition, the user name will be the matrix row names, so we need to store them in the `vector_users` vector:

```
vector_users <- table_wide[, user]
table_wide[, user := NULL]
table_wide[, chunk_user := NULL]
```

In order to have the column names equal to the item names, we need from the `value` prefix. For this purpose, we can use the `substring` function:

```
setnames(x = table_wide,
         old = names(table_wide),
         new = substring(names(table_wide), 7))
```

We need to store the rating matrix within a `recommenderlab` object. For this purpose, we need to convert `table_wide` in a matrix first. In addition, we need to set the row names equal to the user names:

```
matrix_wide <- as.matrix(table_wide)
rownames(matrix_wide) <- vector_users
head(matrix_wide[, 1:6])
```

user	1038	1026	1034	1008	1056	1032
10001	1	1	1	NA	NA	NA
10002	NA	NA	NA	1	1	1
10003	1	1	NA	NA	NA	NA
10004	NA	NA	NA	NA	NA	NA
10005	1	1	1	1	NA	NA
10006	NA	NA	1	NA	NA	NA

The last step is coercing `matrix_wide` into a binary rating matrix using `as`, in the following way:

```
matrix_wide[is.na(matrix_wide)] <- 0
ratings_matrix <- as(matrix_wide, "binaryRatingMatrix")
ratings_matrix
## 5000 x 236 rating matrix of class binaryRatingMatrix with 15191
ratings.
```

Let's take a look at the matrix using `image`:

```
image(ratings_matrix[1:50, 1:50], main = "Binary rating matrix")
```

The following image shows the binary rating matrix:

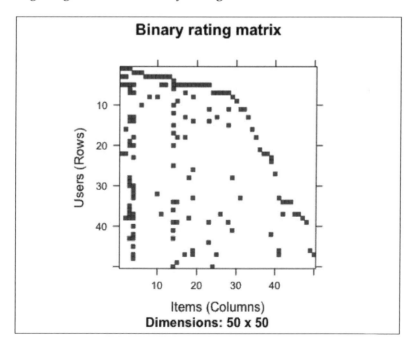

As expected, the matrix is sparse. We can also visualize the distributions of the number of users purchasing an item:

```
n_users <- colCounts(ratings_matrix)
qplot(n_users) + stat_bin(binwidth = 100) + ggtitle("Distribution of the
number of users")
```

The following image displays the distribution of the number of users:

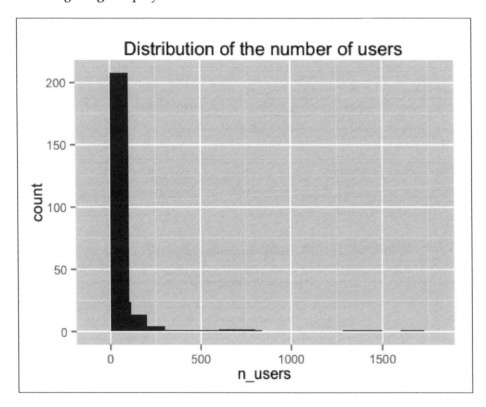

There are some outliers, that is, items purchased by many users. Let's visualize the distribution excluding them:

```
qplot(n_users[n_users < 100]) + stat_bin(binwidth = 10) +
ggtitle("Distribution of the number of users")
```

The following image displays the distribution of the numbers of users:

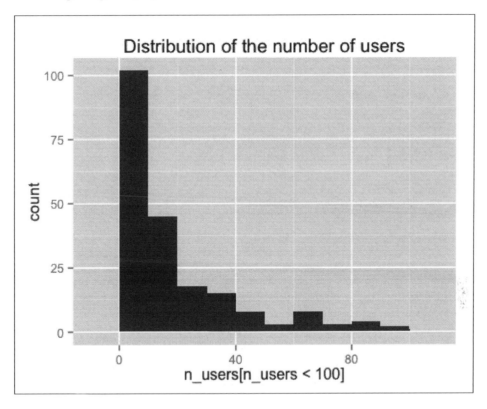

There are many items that have been purchased by a few users only, and we won't recommend them. Since they increase the computational time, we can just remove them by defining a minimum number of purchases, for example, 5:

```
ratings_matrix <- ratings_matrix[, colCounts(ratings_matrix) >= 5]

ratings_matrix

## 5000 x 166 rating matrix of class 'binaryRatingMatrix' with 15043
ratings.
```

Now, we have 166 items, compared to the initial 236. As regards users, we want to recommend items to everyone. However, there might be users that have purchased only items that we removed. Let's check it:

```
sum(rowCounts(ratings_matrix) == 0)
## _15_
```

There are 15 users with no purchases. These purchases should be removed. In addition, users who have purchased just a few items are difficult to deal with. Therefore, we only keep users that have purchased at least five items:

```
ratings_matrix <- ratings_matrix[rowCounts(ratings_matrix) >= 5, ]
ratings_matrix
## 959 x 166 rating matrix of class 'binaryRatingMatrix' with 6816
ratings
```

Extracting item attributes

The `table_in` raw data contains some records starting with A, and they display some information about the items. In order to extract these records, we can convert `table_in` into a data table and extract the rows having A in the first column:

```
table_in <- data.table(table_in)
table_items <- table_in[V1 == "A"]
head(table_items)
```

V1	V2	V3	V4	V5
A	1277	1	NetShow for PowerPoint	/stream
A	1253	1	MS Word Development	/worddev
A	1109	1	TechNet (World Wide Web Edition)	/technet
A	1038	1	SiteBuilder Network Membership	/sbnmember
A	1205	1	Hardware Supprt	/hardwaresupport
A	1076	1	NT Workstation Support	/ntwkssupport

The relevant columns are:

- **V2**: Item ID
- **V4**: Item description
- **V5**: Web page URL

In order to have a more clear table, we can extract and rename them. In addition, we can sort the table by item ID:

```
table_items <- table_items[, c(2, 4, 5), with = FALSE]
setnames(table_items, 1:3, c("id", "description", "url"))
table_items <- table_items[order(id)]
head(table_items)
```

id	description	url
1000	regwiz	/regwiz
1001	Support desktop	/support
1002	End user produced view	/athome
1003	Knowledge base	/kb
1004	Microsoft.com search	/search
1005	Norway	/norge

We need to identify one or more features describing the items. If we look at the table, we can identify two categories of web pages:

- Microsoft product
- Geographic location

We can identify the records containing a geographic location, and consider the remaining as products. For this purpose, we can start defining the field `category` that, at the moment, is equal to `product` for all the records:

```
table_items[, category := "product"]
```

The country code package provides us with the `countrycode_data` object that contains most of the country names. We can define the `name_countries` vector that contains the names of countries and geographic locations. Then, we can categorize as `region` all the records whose description is in `name_countries`:

```
name_countries <- c(countrycode_data$country.name,
            "Taiwan", "UK", "Russia", "Venezuela",
            "Slovenija", "Caribbean", "Netherlands (Holland)",
            "Europe", "Central America", "MS North Africa")
table_items[description %in% name_countries, category := "region"]
```

There are other records containing the word `region`. We can identify them through a regular expression using `grepl`:

```
table_items[grepl("Region", description), category := "region"]
head(table_items)
```

V2	description	url	category
1000	regwiz	/regwiz	product
1001	Support Desktop	/support	product
1002	End User Produced View	/athome	product
1003	Knowledge Base	/kb	product
1004	Microsoft.com Search	/search	product
1005	Norway	/norge	region

Let's take a look at the result and find out the number of items we have for each category:

```
table_items[, list(n_items = .N), by = category]
```

category	n_items
product	248
region	46

About 80 percent of the web pages are products, and the remaining 20 percent are regions.

We are now ready to build recommendation models.

Building the model

This section will show you how to build a recommendation model using item descriptions and user purchases. The model combines item-based collaborative filtering with some information about the items. We will include the item description using a monolithic hybrid system with feature combination. The recommender will learn from the two data sources in two separate stages.

Following the approach described in *Chapter 3, Recommender Systems*, let's split the data into the training and the test set:

```
which_train <- sample(x = c(TRUE, FALSE),
                        size = nrow(ratings_matrix),
                        replace = TRUE,
                        prob = c(0.8, 0.2))
recc_data_train <- ratings_matrix[which_train, ]

recc_data_test <- ratings_matrix[!which_train, ]
```

Now, we can build an IBCF model using `Recommender`. Since the rating matrix is binary, we will set the distance method to `Jaccard`. For more details, look at the *Collaborative filtering on binary data* section in *Chapter 3, Recommender Systems*. The remaining parameters are left to their defaults:

```
recc_model <- Recommender(data = recc_data_train,
                          method = "IBCF",
                          parameter = list(method = "Jaccard"))
```

The engine of IBCF is based on a similarity matrix about the items. The distances are computed from the purchases. The more the number of items purchased by the same users, the more similar they are.

We can extract the matrix from the `sim` element in the slot model. Let's take a look at it:

```
class(recc_model@model$sim)
## dgCMatrix
dim(recc_model@model$sim)
## _166_ and _166_
```

The matrix belongs to the `dgCMatrix` class, and it is square. We can visualize it using `image`:

```
image(recc_model@model$sim)
```

The following image is the output of the preceding code:

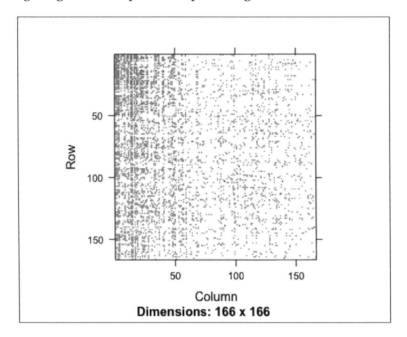

We can't identify any clear pattern, and it's because the items are not sorted. Let's take a look at the range of values:

```
range(recc_model@model$sim)
## _0_ and _1_
```

All the distances are between 0 and 1.

Our target is to combine the distance matrix with the item descriptions, via the following steps:

1. Define a similarity matrix based on the purchases.
2. Define a similarity matrix based on the item descriptions.
3. Combine the two matrices.

Starting from `recc_model`, we can define the purchases similarity matrix. All we need to do is to convert the `dgCMatrix` object into `matrix`:

```
dist_ratings <- as(recc_model@model$sim, "matrix")
```

In order to build the matrix based on item descriptions, we can use the `dist` function. Given that it's based on a category column only, the distance will be as follows:

- 1, if the two items belong to the same category
- 0, if the two items belong to different categories

We need to build a similarity matrix, and we have a distance matrix. Since distances are between 0 and 1, we can just use `1 - dist()`. All the operations are performed within the data table:

```
dist_category <- table_items[, 1 - dist(category == "product")]
class(dist_category)
## dist
```

The `dist_category` raw data is a `dist` object that can be easily converted into a matrix using the `as()` function :

```
dist_category <- as(dist_category, "matrix")
```

Let's compare the dimensions of `dist_category` with `dist_ratings`:

```
dim(dist_category)
## _294_ and _294_
dim(dist_ratings)
## _166_ and _166_
```

The `dist_category` table has more rows and columns, and the reason is that it contains all the items, whereas `dist_ratings` contains only the ones that have been purchased.

In order to combine `dist_category` with `dist_ratings`, we need to have the same items. In addition, they need to be sorted in the same way. We can match them using the item names using these steps:

1. Make sure that both the matrices have the item names in their row and column names.
2. Extract the row and column names from `dist_ratings`.
3. Subset and order `dist_category` according to the names of `dist_ratings`.

The `dist_ratings` table already contains the row and column names. We need to add them to `dist_category`, starting from `table_items`:

```
rownames(dist_category) <- table_items[, id]

colnames(dist_category) <- table_items[, id]
```

Now, it's sufficient to extract the names from `dist_ratings` and subset `dist_category`:

```
vector_items <- rownames(dist_ratings)
dist_category <- dist_category[vector_items, vector_items]
```

Let's check whether the two matrices match:

```
identical(dim(dist_category), dim(dist_ratings))
## TRUE
identical(rownames(dist_category), rownames(dist_ratings))
## TRUE
identical(colnames(dist_category), colnames(dist_ratings))
## TRUE
```

Everything is identical, so they match. Let's take a look at `dist_category`:

```
image(dist_category)
```

The following image is the output of the preceding code:

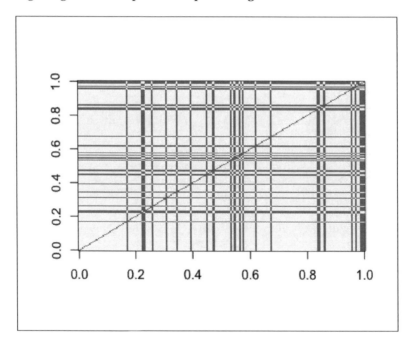

The matrix contains only 0s and 1s, and it's based on two categories, so there are clear patterns. In addition, we can notice that the matrix is symmetric.

We need to combine the two tables, and we can do it with a weighted average. Since `dist_category` takes account of two categories of items only, it's better not to give it too much relevance. For instance, we can set its weight to 25 percent:

```
weight_category <- 0.25
dist_tot <- dist_category * weight_category + dist_ratings * (1 - weight_category)
```

Let's take a look at the `dist_tot` matrix using `image`:

```
image(dist_tot)
```

The following image is the output of the preceding code:

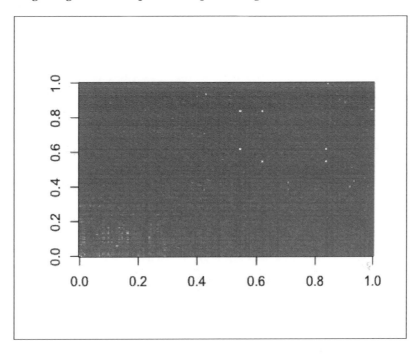

We can see some white dots representing items that are very similar. In addition, we can still see the patterns of `dist_category` in the background.

Now, we can include the new matrix within `recc_model`. For this purpose, it's sufficient to convert `dist_tot` into `dgCMatrix` and insert it in `recc_model`:

```
recc_model@model$sim <- as(dist_tot, "dgCMatrix")
recc_model@model$sim <- as(dist_tot, "dgCMatrix")
```

As shown in *Chapter 3, Recommender Systems,* we can recommend items using `predict()`:

```
n_recommended <- 10
recc_predicted <- predict(object = recc_model,
                          newdata = recc_data_test,
                          n = n_recommended)
```

The `itemLabels` slot of `recc_predicted` contains the item names, that is, their code:

```
head(recc_predicted@itemLabels)
```

```
1038, 1026, 1034, 1008, 1056 and 1032
```

In order to display the item description, we can use `table_items`. All we need to do is make sure that the items are ordered in the same way as `itemLabels`. For this purpose, we will prepare a data frame containing the item information. We will also make sure that it's sorted in the same way as the item labels using the following steps:

1. Define a data frame having a column with the ordered item labels.

   ```
   table_labels <- data.frame(id = recc_predicted@itemLabels)
   ```

2. Left-join between `table_labels` and `table_items`. Note the argument `sort = FALSE` that does not let us re-sort the table:

   ```
   table_labels <- merge(table_labels, table_items,
                   by = "id", all.x = TRUE, all.y = FALSE,
                   sort = FALSE)
   ```

3. Convert the description from factor to character:

   ```
   descriptions <- as(table_labels$description, "character")
   ```

Let's take a look at `table_labels`:

```
head(table_labels)
```

id	description	url	category
1038	SiteBuilder Network Membership	/sbnmember	product
1026	Internet Site Construction for Developers	/sitebuilder	product
1034	Internet Explorer	/ie	product
1008	Free Downloads	/msdownload	product
1056	sports	/sports	product
1032	Games	/games	product

As expected, the table contains the description of the items. Now, we are able to extract the recommendations. For instance, we can do it for the first user:

```
recc_user_1 <- recc_predicted@items[[1]]
items_user_1 <- descriptions[recc_user_1]
head(items_user_1)
```

Windows family of OSs, Support Desktop, Knowledge Base, Microsoft.com Search, Products, and Windows 95.

Now, we can define a table with the recommendations to all users. Each column corresponds to a user and each row to a recommended item. Having set n_recommended to 10, the table should have 10 rows. For this purpose, we can use sapply() For each element of recc_predicted@items, we identify the related item descriptions.

However, the number of recommended items per user is a number between 1 and 10, which is not the same for each user. In order to define a structured table with 10 rows, we need the same number of elements for each user. For this reason, we will replace the missing recommendations with empty strings. We can obtain it by replicating the empty string with rep():

```
recc_matrix <- sapply(recc_predicted@items, function(x){
  recommended <- descriptions[x]
  c(recommended, rep("", n_recommended - length(recommended)))
})
dim(recc_matrix)
## _10_ and _191_
```

Let's take a look at the recommendations for the first three users:

```
head(recc_matrix[, 1:3])
```

Windows family of OSs	Products	Developer workshop
Support Desktop	MS Word	SiteBuilder Network Membership
Knowledge Base	isapi	isapi
Microsoft.com Search	regwiz	Microsoft.com Search
Products	Windows family of OSs	Windows Family of OSs
Windows 95	Microsoft.com Search	Web Site Builder's Gallery

We can notice that some items have been recommended to the three of them: Products and Support Desktop. Therefore, we suspect that some items are much more likely to be recommended.

Just like we did in *Chapter 3, Recommender Systems*, we can explore the output. For each item, we can count how many times it has been recommended:

```
table_recomm_per_item <- table(recc_matrix)
recomm_per_item <- as(table_recomm_per_item, "numeric")
```

In order to visualize the result, we bin_recomm_per_item using cut():

```
bin_recomm_per_item <- cut(recomm_per_item,
                  breaks = c(0, 10, 20, 100,
                              max(recomm_per_item)))
```

Using qplot, we can visualize the recomm_per_item distribution:

```
qplot(bin_recomm_per_item) + ggtitle("Recommendations per item")
```

The following image displays the recommendations per item:

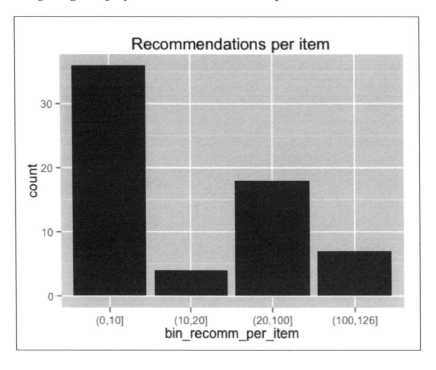

Most of the items have been recommended 10 times or fewer, and a few of them have more than 100 recommendations. The distribution has a long tail.

We can also identify the most popular items by sorting `recomm_per_item`:

```
recomm_per_item_sorted <- sort(table_recomm_per_item,
                               decreasing = TRUE)
                               recomm_per_item_top <-
                               head(recomm_per_item_sorted, n = 4)
table_top <- data.frame(
  name = names(recomm_per_item_top),
  n_recomm = recomm_per_item_top)
table_top
```

name	n_recomm
Internet Explorer	126
Windows Family of OSs	120
Knowledge Base	118
Products	115

In this section, we built and explored a hybrid recommender model. The next step is to evaluate it and optimize its parameters.

Evaluating and optimizing the model

This section will show you how to evaluate the performance of our recommender. Starting from the evaluation, we can try some parameter configurations and choose the one performing the best. For more details, see *Chapter 4, Evaluating the Recommender Systems*.

The following are the steps to evaluate and optimize the model:

- Build a function that evaluates the model given a parameter configuration
- Use the function to test different parameter configurations and pick the best one

Let's go through these steps in detail.

Building a function to evaluate the model

This section will show you how to define a function that:

1. Sets up cross validation using the *k*-fold.
2. Builds a hybrid IBCF.

3. Recommends the items to the users in the test sets.

4. Evaluates the recommendation.

The inputs of our function are as follows:

- **Data**: This is the rating matrix table with the item description
- **k-fold parameters**: This is the number of folds, the number of items to keep in the test set
- **Model parameters**: This is the number of nearest neighbors, weight to the description-based distance, number of items to recommend

Let's define the function arguments. You can find the description of each argument as a comment next to its name:

```
evaluateModel <- function (
  # data inputs
  ratings_matrix, # rating matrix
  table_items, # item description table
  # K-fold parameters
  n_fold = 10, # number of folds
  items_to_keep = 4, # number of items to keep in the test set
  # model parameters
  number_neighbors = 30, # number of nearest neighbors
  weight_description = 0.2, # weight to the item description-based
  distance
  items_to_recommend = 10 # number of items to recommend
){
  # build and evaluate the model
}
```

Now, we can walk through the function body step by step. For a more detailed explanation, see the previous section and *Chapter 4, Evaluating the Recommender Systems*:

1. Using the `evaluationScheme()` function, set-up a *k*-fold. The parameters *k* and given are set according to the inputs `n_fold` and `items_to_keep`, respectively. The `set.seed(1)` command makes sure that the example is reproducible, that is, the random component will be the same if repeated:

    ```
    set.seed(1)
    eval_sets <- evaluationScheme(data = ratings_matrix,
                                  method = "cross-validation",
    ```

```
                                    k = n_fold,
                                    given = items_to_keep)
```

2. Using `Recommender()`, build an IBCF defining the distance function as `Jaccard` and the *k* argument as the `number_neighbors` input:

```
recc_model <- Recommender(data = getData(eval_sets, "train"),
                          method = "IBCF",
                          parameter = list(method = "Jaccard",
                          k = number_neighbors))
```

3. Extract the rating-based distance matrix from the `recc_model` model:

```
dist_ratings <- as(recc_model@model$sim, "matrix")
vector_items <- rownames(dist_ratings)
```

4. Starting from the `table_items` input, define the description-based distance matrix:

```
dist_category <- table_items[, 1 - as.matrix(dist(category ==
"product"))]
rownames(dist_category) <- table_items[, id]
colnames(dist_category) <- table_items[, id]
dist_category <- dist_category[vector_items, vector_items]
```

5. Define the distance matrix combining `dist_ratings` and `dist_category`. The combination is a weighted average, and the weight is defined by the `weight_description` input:

```
dist_tot <- dist_category * weight_description +
   dist_ratings * (1 - weight_description)
recc_model@model$sim <- as(dist_tot, "dgCMatrix")
```

6. Predict the test set users with known purchases. Since we are using a table with 0 and 1 ratings only, we can specify that we predict the top n recommendations with the argument `type = "topNList"`. The argument n, defining the number of items to recommend, comes from the `items_to_recommend` input:

```
eval_prediction <- predict(object = recc_model,
                           newdata = getData(eval_sets,
                           "known"),
                           n = items_to_recommend,
                           type = "topNList")
```

7. Evaluate the model performance using `calcPredictionAccuracy()`.
    Specifying `byUser = FALSE`, we have a table with the average indices such
    as precision and recall:

    ```
    eval_accuracy <- calcPredictionAccuracy(
      x = eval_prediction,
      data = getData(eval_sets, "unknown"),
      byUser = FALSE,
      given = items_to_recommend)
    ```

8. The function output is the `eval_accuracy` table:

    ```
    return(eval_accuracy)
    ```

9. Now, we can test our function:

    ```
    model_evaluation <- evaluateModel(ratings_matrix = ratings_matrix,
                                      table_items = table_items)

    model_evaluation
    ```

index	value
TP	2
FP	8
FN	1
TN	145
precision	19%
recall	64%
TPR	64%
FPR	5%

You can find a detailed description of the indices in *Chapter 4, Evaluating the Recommender Systems*.

In this section, we defined a function evaluating our model with given settings. This function will help us with parameter optimization.

Optimizing the model parameters

Starting with our `evaluateModel()` function, we can optimize the model parameters. In this section, we will optimize these parameters:

*   `number_neighbors`: This is the number of nearest neighbors of IBCF

*   `weight_description`: This is the weight given to the description-based distance

Although we could optimize other parameters, we will just leave them to their defaults, for the sake of simplicity.

Our recommender model combines IBCF with the item descriptions. Therefore, it's a good practice to optimize IBCF first, that is, the `number_neighbors` parameter.

First, we have to decide which values we want to test. We take account of k, that is, at most, half of the items, that is, about `80`. On the other hand, we exclude values that are smaller than 4, since the algorithm would be too unstable. Setting a granularity of `2`, we can generate a vector with the values to test:

```
nn_to_test <- seq(4, 80, by = 2)
```

Now, we can measure the performance depending on `number_neighbors`. Since we are optimizing the IBCF part only, we will set weight_description = 0. Using `lapply`, we can build a list of elements that contain the performance for each value of `nn_to_test`:

```
list_performance <- lapply(
  X = nn_to_test,
  FUN = function(nn){
    evaluateModel(ratings_matrix = ratings_matrix,
                  table_items = table_items,
                  number_neighbors = nn,
                  weight_description = 0)
})
```

Let's take a look at the first element of the list:

```
list_performance[[1]]
```

name	value
TP	1.663
FP	8.337
FN	1.683
TN	144.3
precision	0.1663
recall	0.5935
TPR	0.5935
FPR	0.05449

The first element contains all the performance metrics. In order to evaluate our model, we can use the precision and recall. See *Chapter 4, Evaluating the Recommender Systems* for more information.

We can extract a vector of precisions (or recalls) using `sapply`:

```
sapply(list_performance, "[[", "precision")^t
```

```
0.1663, 0.1769, 0.1769, 0.175, 0.174, 0.1808, 0.176, 0.1779, 0.1788,
0.1788, 0.1808, 0.1817, 0.1817, 0.1837, 0.1846, 0.1837, 0.1827, 0.1817,
0.1827, 0.1827, 0.1817, 0.1808, 0.1817, 0.1808, 0.1808, 0.1827, 0.1827,
0.1837, 0.1827, 0.1808, 0.1798, 0.1798, 0.1798, 0.1798, 0.1798, 0.1798,
0.1788, 0.1788 and 0.1788
```

In order to analyze the output, we can define a table whose columns are `nn_to_test`, precisions, and recalls:

```
table_performance <- data.table(
  nn = nn_to_test,
  precision = sapply(list_performance, "[[", "precision"),
  recall = sapply(list_performance, "[[", "recall")
)
```

In addition, we can define a performance index that we will optimize. The performance index can be a weighted average between the precision and the recall. The weights depend on the use case, so we can just leave them to 50 percent:

```
weight_precision <- 0.5
```

```
table_performance[
    performance := precision * weight_precision + recall * (1 -
    weight_precision)]
head(table_performance)
```

nn	precision	recall	performance
4	0.1663	0.5935	0.3799
6	0.1769	0.621	0.399
8	0.1769	0.5973	0.3871
10	0.175	0.5943	0.3846
12	0.174	0.5909	0.3825
14	0.1808	0.6046	0.3927

The precision is the percentage of recommended items that have been purchased, and the recall is the percentage of purchased items that have been recommended.

The `table_performance` table contains all the evaluation metrics. Starting with it, we can build charts that help us identify the optimal `nn`.

Before building the charts, let's define the `convertIntoPercent()` function that we will use within the `ggplot2` functions:

```
convertIntoPercent <- function(x){
  paste0(round(x * 100), "%")
}
```

We are ready to build the charts. The first chart is about the precision based on nn. We can build it using these functions:

- `qplot`: This builds the scatterplot.
- `geom_smooth`: This adds a smoothing line.
- `scale_y_continuous`: This changes the y scale. In our case, we just want to display the percentage.

The following command consists of the preceding points:

```
qplot(table_performance[, nn], table_performance[, precision]) +
geom_smooth() + scale_y_continuous(labels = convertIntoPercent)
```

The following image is the output of the preceding code:

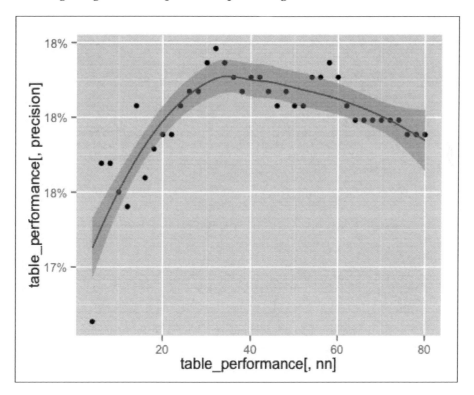

The smoothed line grows until the global maximum, which is around `nn = 35`, slowly decreases. This index expresses the percentage of recommendations that have been successful, so it's useful when there are high costs associated with advertising.

Let's take a look at the recall, using the same commands:

```
qplot(table_performance[, nn], table_performance[, recall]) +
geom_smooth() + scale_y_continuous(labels = convertIntoPercent)
```

The following image is the output of the preceding screenshot:

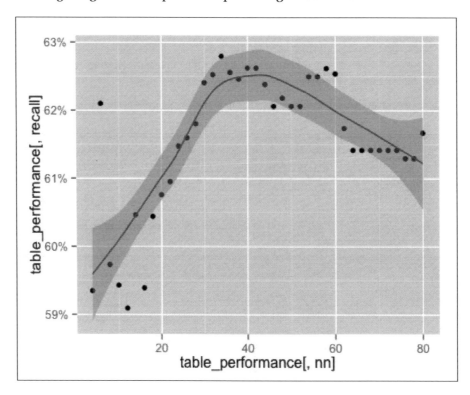

The maximum recall is around `nn = 40`. This index expresses the percentage of purchases that we recommended, so it's useful if we want to be sure to predict most of the purchases.

The performance takes account of the precision and the recall at the same time. Let's take a look at it:

```
qplot(table_performance[, nn], table_performance[, performance]) +
geom_smooth() + scale_y_continuous(labels = convertIntoPercent)
```

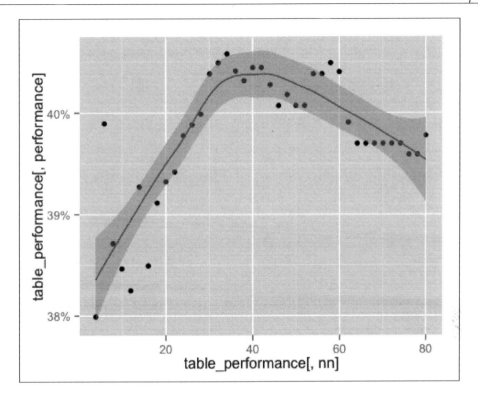

The optimal performances are between 30 and 45. We can identify the best nn using `which.max`:

```
row_best <- which.max(table_performance$performance)
number_neighbors_opt <- table_performance[row_best, nn]
number_neighbors_opt
## _34_
```

The optimal value is 34. We optimized the IBCF parameter, and the next step is determining the weight of the item description component. First, let's define the weights to try. The possible weights range between 0 and 1, and we just need to set the granularity, for instance, 0.05:

```
wd_to_try <- seq(0, 1, by = 0.05)
```

Using `lapply`, we can test the recommender based on the weight:

```
list_performance <- lapply(
  X = wd_to_try,
  FUN = function(wd) {
```

```
    evaluateModel(ratings_matrix = ratings_matrix,
              table_items = table_items,
              number_neighbors = number_neighbors_opt,
              weight_description = wd)
})
```

Just like we did earlier, we can build a table containing precisions, recalls, and performances:

```
table_performance <- data.table(
  wd = wd_to_try,
  precision = sapply(list_performance, "[[", "precision"),
  recall = sapply(list_performance, "[[", "recall")
)
```

```
table_performance[
    performance := precision * weight_precision + recall * (1 - weight_
precision)]
```

Now, we can visualize the performance based on the weight through a chart:

```
qplot(table_performance[, wd], table_performance[, performance]) +
geom_smooth() + scale_y_continuous(labels = convertIntoPercent)
```

The following image is the output of the preceding command:

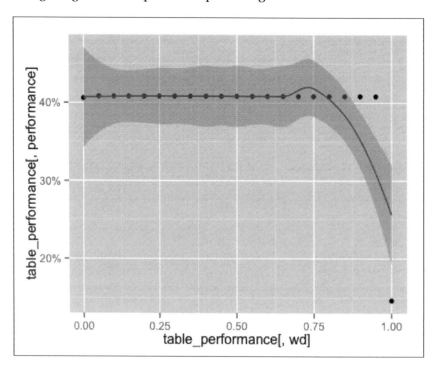

The performance is the same for each point, with the exception of the extremes. Therefore, the smoothing line is not useful.

We have the best performance that takes account of both ratings and descriptions. The extreme **0.00** corresponds to pure IBCF, and it performs slightly worse than the hybrid. The model in the extreme **1.00** is based on the item description only, and that's why it performs so badly.

The reason why the performance doesn't change much is that the item description is based on a binary feature only. If we add other features, we will see a greater impact.

This section showed you how to optimize our recommendation algorithm on the basis of two parameters. A next step could be optimizing on the basis of the remaining IBCF parameters and improving the item description.

Summary

This chapter showed you how to apply the techniques in a real-life context. Starting with raw unstructured data, we built a rating matrix, which is the input of collaborative filtering. In addition, we extracted the item description, which improved the performance of our model. Using performance evaluations, we optimized the model parameters. The same approach can be applied in real-life contexts, if properly refined.

This book is a path that shows, first, the basics of machine learning and then a practical application. After having read this book, you will be able to deal with real-life challenges, identifying the most appropriate recommendation solution. Thank you for following until this point.

If you have any queries, don't hesitate to contact us.

References

To learn more about recommender systems and machine learning use the following references:

- *The Recommender Systems: An Introduction* by *Dietmar Jannach, Markus Zanker, Alexander Felfernig,* and *Gerhard Friedrich*
- *Recommender Systems Handbook* by *Francesco Ricci, Lior Rokach, Bracha Shapira,* and *Paul B. Kantor*
- *An Introduction to Statistical Learning with Applications in R* by *Gareth James, Daniela Witten, Trevor Hastie,* and *Robert Tibshirani*
- `https://en.wikipedia.org/wiki/Precision_and_recall`
- The online course, *Machine Learning,* by *Andrew NG* at `https://www.coursera.org/`

Index

Thank you for buying
Building a Recommendation System with R

About Packt Publishing

Packt, pronounced 'packed', published its first book, *Mastering phpMyAdmin for Effective MySQL Management*, in April 2004, and subsequently continued to specialize in publishing highly focused books on specific technologies and solutions.

Our books and publications share the experiences of your fellow IT professionals in adapting and customizing today's systems, applications, and frameworks. Our solution-based books give you the knowledge and power to customize the software and technologies you're using to get the job done. Packt books are more specific and less general than the IT books you have seen in the past. Our unique business model allows us to bring you more focused information, giving you more of what you need to know, and less of what you don't.

Packt is a modern yet unique publishing company that focuses on producing quality, cutting-edge books for communities of developers, administrators, and newbies alike. For more information, please visit our website at www.packtpub.com.

About Packt Open Source

In 2010, Packt launched two new brands, Packt Open Source and Packt Enterprise, in order to continue its focus on specialization. This book is part of the Packt Open Source brand, home to books published on software built around open source licenses, and offering information to anybody from advanced developers to budding web designers. The Open Source brand also runs Packt's Open Source Royalty Scheme, by which Packt gives a royalty to each open source project about whose software a book is sold.

Writing for Packt

We welcome all inquiries from people who are interested in authoring. Book proposals should be sent to author@packtpub.com. If your book idea is still at an early stage and you would like to discuss it first before writing a formal book proposal, then please contact us; one of our commissioning editors will get in touch with you.

We're not just looking for published authors; if you have strong technical skills but no writing experience, our experienced editors can help you develop a writing career, or simply get some additional reward for your expertise.

Mastering Predictive Analytics
with R

ISBN: 978-1-78398-280-6   Paperback: 414 pages

Master the craft of predictive modeling by developing strategy, intuition, and a solid foundation in essential concepts

1. Grasp the major methods of predictive modeling and move beyond black box thinking to a deeper level of understanding.

2. Leverage the flexibility and modularity of R to experiment with a range of different techniques and data types.

3. Packed with practical advice and tips explaining important concepts and best practices to help you understand quickly and easily.

Learning Data Mining with R

ISBN: 978-1-78398-210-3   Paperback: 314 pages

Develop key skills and techniques with R to create and customize data mining algorithms

1. Develop a sound strategy for solving predictive modeling problems using the most popular data mining algorithms.

2. Gain understanding of the major methods of predictive modeling.

3. Packed with practical advice and tips to help you get to grips with data mining.

Please check **www.PacktPub.com** for information on our titles

Mastering Scientific Computing with R

ISBN: 978-1-78355-525-3   Paperback: 432 pages

Employ professional quantitative methods to answer scientific questions with a powerful open source data analysis environment

1. Perform publication-quality science using R.

2. Use some of R's most powerful and least known features to solve complex scientific computing problems.

3. Learn how to create visual illustrations of scientific results.

R for Data Science

ISBN: 978-1-78439-086-0   Paperback: 364 pages

Learn and explore the fundamentals of data science with R

1. Familiarize yourself with R programming packages and learn how to utilize them effectively.

2. Learn how to detect different types of data mining sequences.

3. A step-by-step guide to understanding R scripts and the ramifications of your changes.

Please check **www.PacktPub.com** for information on our titles

38169601R00090

Made in the USA
San Bernardino, CA
01 September 2016